FAST and FRESH

FAST and FRESH

quick recipes for busy lives

LOUISE PICKFORD

with photography by Peter Cassidy

RYLAND PETERS & SMALL
LONDON • NEW YORK

AUTHOR'S ACKNOWLEDGMENTS

Thank you to everyone at Ryland Peters & Small for their continued support, and also to my husband, who tastes and assesses everything I cook and still remains impartial.

Senior Designer Susan Downing
Commissioning Editor Elsa Petersen-Schepelern
Editors Katherine Steer and Lesley Malkin
US Editor Jennifer Herman
Production Patricia Harrington
Art Director Gabriella Le Grazie
Publishing Director Alison Starling

Food Stylist Julz Beresford
Prop Stylist Helen Trent
Indexer Hilary Bird

First published in 2003.
This updated edition published in 2017
by **Ryland Peters & Small**
20–21 Jockey's Fields
London
WC1R 4BW
and
341 E 116th St
New York
NY 10029
www.rylandpeters.com

ISBN: 978-1-84975-857-4

10 9 8 7 6 5 4 3 2

Text © Louise Pickford 2003, 2017
Design and photographs © Ryland Peters & Small 2003, 2017

A CIP record for this book is available from the British Library.
The original US edition was catalogued as follows:
Library of Congress Cataloging-in-Publication Data

Pickford, Louise.
  Fast & fresh : quick recipes for busy lives / Louise Pickford ; with photography by Peter Cassidy.
      p. cm.
Includes index.
  ISBN 1-84172-404-1
  1. Quick and easy cookery. I. Title: Fast and fresh. II. Title.
TX833.5 .P533 2003
641.5'55--dc21
                          2002013769

Notes

Both British (Metric) and American (Imperial plus US cups) measurements are included in these recipes for your convenience, however it is very important to work with one set of measurements only and not alternate between the two within a recipe. All spoon measurements are level – a teaspoon is 5 ml and a tablespoon is 15 ml.

All eggs are UK large and US extra-large, unless otherwise specified. Uncooked or partly cooked eggs should not be served to the very young, the very old, those with a compromised immune systems, or to pregnant women.

Ovens should be preheated to the specified temperatures. If using a fan-assisted/convection oven, adjust temperatures according to the manufacturer's instructions.

Printed and bound in China.

East Sussex
County Council

Eastbourne Library
Grove Road, Eastbourne, BN21 4TL.

Account: **0542

Fast and fresh : quick recipes for busy
lives
Due date: 28/02/23

Total items borrowed: 1

07/02/23 2:28 PM

CONTENTS

Fast Food for Busy Lives 6

Appetizers 8
Vegetarian and Sides 18
Eggs and Cheese 34
Fish and Seafood 48
Poultry and Meat 66
Pasta, Rice, Noodles 88
Pizza and Bread 104
Desserts and Drinks 116

The Basics 140
Index 144

FAST FOOD FOR BUSY LIVES

This is a recipe book for today's cook and will help you to make the best use of time when it comes to preparing a meal. Although in an ideal world it would be nice to saunter at our leisure through food markets or shop at individual suppliers, reality rarely provides us with such luxury. More usual is a quick dash to the supermarket on the way home.

Once you're in the kitchen, recipes must be fuss-free – no complicated sauces or stocks that take several hours to prepare, but just making the most of good-quality, seasonal produce. I cannot over-emphasize the importance of shopping for seasonal produce. Vegetables that were still in the ground just a few hours ago would be fantastic, but for most of us this is a bit of a pipe dream. However, buying locally grown produce is both possible and advisable – not only are they likely to taste better than those that have been picked under-ripe and transported right half way round the world, but also they will most likely be far cheaper too.

To me, cooking is more than purely sustenance – it is also a love and passion for creating flavours that delight and dishes that satisfy. It is the pleasure of sitting down with friends or family, sharing thoughts and anecdotes, or just enjoying the food and company with a glass of wine. Cooking should be fun, not a chore.

Because most of us want a quick fix at the end of a busy day, we often opt for fast or convenience foods that will fill the gap – but do these ever truly satisfy us? What if you could shop, prepare, and cook a delicious meal in the time it takes to order and collect that takeaway/takeout? With Fast & Fresh you can.

APPETIZERS

Sometimes, especially when I'm in a hurry, I might skip the appetizer altogether and just concentrate on the main plate – and a dessert, of course.

Other times, I make a quick antipasti with my favourite things from the deli counter – perhaps Parma ham or prosciutto, salami and other cold cuts – plus a dish of olives, or toast and dips.

A simple salad also makes a great start to a meal – just crisp green leaves and a vinaigrette, either plain or with blue cheese added. Or something exotic, such as the pea shoots with wasabi-flavoured mayonnaise on page 14. Or use the same wasabi mayonnaise as a dip for some raw fresh vegetables or crudités.

Often, however, I think that small-plate appetizers are the most exciting part of a meal. You can turn them into a sharing feast if you like – I sometimes make a selection of dishes, so people can dip in, as you do with mezze or tapas. This is a fun way to eat and although you may need a little more time to prepare a selection of dishes, there is little else to do later other than enjoy the meal.

Thai fish, prawn/shrimp or crab cakes are quick and easy to make – perfect as an appetizer, or as a spicy snack with cocktails. If you have time, marinate the prawn/shrimp mixture for 30 minutes or so. I keep a few bottles of chilli/chili jam at home, but you can use a prepared chilli/chili sauce if you prefer.

THAI SHRIMP CAKES
with chilli/chili jam

500 g/1 lb. uncooked, shelled and deveined prawns/shrimp

4 lime leaves, very finely chopped, or grated zest of 1 lime

4 spring onions/scallions, finely chopped

2 tablespoons chopped fresh coriander/cilantro

1 egg

1 tablespoon Thai fish sauce

50 g/⅓ cup rice flour or cornstarch

peanut or safflower oil, for frying

chilli/chili jam (below) or sweet chilli/chili sauce, to serve

CHILLI/CHILI JAM

500 g/1 lb. ripe tomatoes, coarsely chopped

3–4 red chillies/chiles, coarsely chopped

2 garlic cloves, chopped

1 teaspoon grated fresh ginger

2 tablespoons light soy sauce

250 g/1¼ cups palm sugar or brown sugar

100 ml/½ cup white wine vinegar

½ teaspoon sea salt

2 preserving jars, about 200 ml/1 cup each, sterilized

serves 6 (makes 24 cakes)

To make the chilli/chili jam, put the tomatoes, chillies/chiles and garlic in a food processor and purée until smooth. Transfer to a saucepan, add the ginger, soy sauce, sugar, vinegar and salt, and bring to the boil. Cook for 30–35 minutes, stirring occasionally until thick and glossy.

Warm the jars in a low oven, pour in the thickened jam and let cool completely. Seal and store in the refrigerator.

To make the prawn/shrimp cakes, put the prawns/shrimp into a food processor and blend to a purée. Add the lime leaves, spring onions/scallions, coriander/cilantro, egg, fish sauce and rice flour, blend briefly and transfer to a bowl. Using damp hands, shape the mixture into 24 patties, 5 cm/2 inches diameter.

Pour 1-cm/½-inch depth of the oil in a frying pan/skillet, heat for 1 minute over medium heat, then add the cakes, spaced apart. Cook in batches for 2 minutes on each side until golden brown. Remove and drain on paper towels and keep them warm in a low oven while you cook the remainder. Serve with chilli/chili jam or sweet chilli/chili sauce.

This version of baba ganoush, the spicy Middle Eastern aubergine/eggplant purée, uses yogurt instead of the traditional tahini. The aubergine/eggplant should be charred well to achieve the best smoky flavour.

YOGURT BABA GANOUSH DIP

1 large aubergine/eggplant
2 tablespoons extra virgin olive oil
1 teaspoon ground cumin
200 ml/1 cup plain yogurt
2 spring onions/scallions, finely chopped
1 tablespoon freshly squeezed lemon juice
sea salt and freshly ground black pepper
toasted pitta/pita bread, to serve

serves 6

Cut the aubergine/eggplant lengthways into thin slices, about 2 mm/⅛ inch. Put the oil in a small bowl, add the cumin, salt and pepper, mix well, then brush all over the aubergine/eggplant.

Cook on a preheated stove-top grill pan or under a hot grill/broiler for 3–4 minutes on each side until charred and tender. Let cool, then chop finely.

Put the yogurt in a bowl, then stir in the aubergine/eggplant, spring onions/scallions and lemon juice. Taste and adjust the seasoning with salt and pepper. Serve in bowls or on plates, with toasted pitta/pita bread for dipping.

If you can't find the Greek dip tzatziki, make chive cheese instead by snipping fresh chives into cream cheese. This topping can also be used as a sandwich filling.

SMOKED SALMON BRUSCHETTA
with rocket/arugula and tzatziki

4 thick slices of sourdough bread
1 large garlic clove, halved
2 tablespoons extra virgin olive oil, plus extra to serve
250 g/8 oz. tzatziki
250 g/8 oz. smoked salmon slices
a handful of rocket/arugula
freshly ground black pepper

serves 6

Toast the bread on a preheated stove-top grill pan or under a hot grill/broiler. While still hot, rub all over with the garlic and sprinkle with oil. Top each slice with a large spoonful of tzatziki, then pile on the salmon and rocket/arugula. Season with pepper and serve sprinkled with a little extra oil.

HOMEMADE HERB CHEESE

400 g/1¾ cups plain yogurt

100 ml/¼ cup double/heavy cream

1 garlic clove, crushed

3 tablespoons chopped fresh basil

3 tablespoons chopped mixed fresh
  herbs, including dill, marjoram,
  parsley and thyme leaves

sea salt and freshly ground black
  pepper

wholemeal/whole wheat or soda
  bread (page 112)

a piece of muslin/cheesecloth,
30 cm/12 inches square

serves 4–6

Put all the ingredients in a bowl and stir well. Line a second bowl with a large piece of muslin/cheesecloth and spoon in the yogurt mixture. Pull up the ends of the cheesecloth to form a bag and tie tightly with kitchen string.

Hang the bag over the bowl so the liquid can drain from the yogurt. Leave in the refrigerator overnight. Unwrap the bag and transfer the cheese to a serving bowl. Serve with wholemeal/whole wheat or soda bread.

Pea shoots are the tendrils and baby leaves of mangetouts/snowpeas. You often see them in Chinese and Southeast Asian markets, but if you can't find any, use watercress instead. It gives a delicious peppery flavour, which mirrors the fiery spice of wasabi.

PEA SHOOT SALAD
with wasabi mayonnaise

100 g/4 oz. dried Chinese egg
  noodles, soaked and drained
  according to the directions on the
  package

200 g/8 oz. pea shoots or watercress

125 g/4 oz. radishes, sliced and cut
  into strips

sea salt

peanut or safflower oil, for deep-frying

wasabi mayonnaise dressing

1 recipe Mayonnaise (page 142)

1 tablespoon wasabi paste

2 tablespoons rice wine vinegar

serves 4

Heat 5 cm/2 inches of oil in deep saucepan to 180°C (350°F) on a sugar/candy thermometer (or a cube of bread crisps and browns in 30 seconds). Break the noodles into 5-cm/2-inch lengths and add to the oil in 4 batches (be careful because the fat will foam up as the noodles are added). Fry for 1–2 minutes until crisp. Drain on paper towels and sprinkle with salt.

Mix the mayonnaise, wasabi and vinegar in a bowl. Add the pea shoots or watercress and radishes and toss until evenly coated. Top with the noodles and serve at once.

Yogurt-crusted chicken threaded onto skewers makes ideal finger food for buffets and cocktail parties. The yogurt tenderizes the chicken and helps the lemon soak into the meat. For the best flavour, cook them on a barbecue – the yogurt becomes delicious and slightly crunchy.

CHICKEN + LEMON SKEWERS

500 g/1 lb. skinless, boneless chicken breasts

marinade

250 g/1 cup plain yogurt

2 tablespoons extra virgin olive oil

2 garlic cloves, crushed

grated zest and freshly squeezed juice of 1 unwaxed lemon

1–2 teaspoons chilli/chili powder

1 tablespoon chopped fresh coriander/cilantro

sea salt and freshly ground black pepper

12 bamboo skewers, soaked in cold water for 30 minutes

serves 4

Cut the chicken lengthways into 2-mm/⅛ inch strips and put in a shallow ceramic dish.

Put all the marinade ingredients in a bowl, stir well, and pour over the chicken. Turn to coat, cover and let marinate in the refrigerator overnight.

The next day, thread the chicken onto the soaked bamboo skewers, zig-zagging the meat back and forth as you go.

Cook on a preheated barbecue or under a hot grill/broiler for 3–4 minutes on each side until charred and tender. Let cool slightly before serving.

VEGETARIAN + SIDES

This chapter is about cooking vegetables as well as cooking vegetarian food.

You will reap great rewards by buying seasonal produce. Though most of us aren't fortunate enough to have a vegetable garden, there are farmers' or organic markets which offer the best chance of buying ingredients harvested within hours of purchase.

If you have good-quality produce, the rest is easy – add a single herb or spice to compliment a particular vegetable and make a side dish that tastes wonderful and will go well with a whole range of meat and fish.

Living with a non-meat-eater means I eat very little meat myself and, although we both eat fish, vegetable dishes form the basis of our diet. This chapter is great for vegetarians looking for quick and simple recipes, but I hope it will also surprise and inspire many who feel a meat-free meal can be a bit dull.

I often hear it said that vegetarian food is all well and good if you have plenty of time, but that's no help if you're in hurry. Let me dispel that myth and prove it is just as quick and easy to make a meat-free meal as it is to make any other.

Tabbouleh, the fresh parsley salad from Lebanon, is based on bulghur wheat. This one is made with couscous, the fine Moroccan pasta, now available in an instant version – you just soak it in water or stock for 10 minutes or so.

FRAGRANT HERB COUSCOUS SALAD

300 g/1½ cups couscous
freshly squeezed juice of 1 lemon
2 tablespoons chopped fresh basil
2 tablespoons chopped fresh coriander/cilantro
2 tablespoons chopped fresh mint
2 tablespoons chopped fresh parsley
sea salt and freshly ground black pepper
2 lemons, halved, to serve (optional)
fragrant garlic oil
1 whole head of garlic, cloves separated
2 bay leaves
600 ml/2¾ cups extra virgin olive oil

serves 4

To make the fragrant garlic oil, peel the cloves and put them in a saucepan. Add the bay leaves and oil and heat gently for 15 minutes until the garlic has softened. Don't let the garlic brown. Let cool, remove and mash the garlic cloves, then return them to the oil. Refrigerate until required. Use 150 ml/1¼ cups for this recipe and reserve the remainder.

Put the couscous in a bowl, add water to cover by 5 cm/2 inches and let soak for 10 minutes.

Drain the soaked couscous, shaking the seive/strainer well to remove any excess water. Transfer to a bowl, add the fragrant garlic oil, lemon juice, chopped basil, coriander/cilantro, mint and parsley. Season with salt and pepper, then set aside to develop the flavours until ready to serve. Serve with halved lemons, if using.

1 tablespoon sesame oil

1 onion, sliced

200 g/8 oz. green/string beans

12 oz. deep-fried tofu, sliced

2 tablespoons sweet chilli/chili sauce

a handful basil leaves, preferably Thai

2 tablespoons sesame seeds, toasted in a dry frying pan/skillet

SAUCE

400 ml/1¾ cups coconut milk

300 ml/1½ cups Vegetable Stock (page 143)

2 stalks of lemongrass, sliced crosswise

1 tablespoon Thai fish sauce

8 lime leaves, sliced, or grated lime zest

2 garlic cloves, chopped

3 cm/1 inch fresh ginger, peeled and grated

serves 4

Deep-fried tofu cakes are available from Asian markets or wholefood stores where they can be found in the refrigerator. You can substitute regular firm tofu, cut into cubes instead.

STIR-FRIED TOFU
with chilli coconut sauce

Put all the sauce ingredients in a saucepan, bring to the boil and simmer for 20 minutes until reduced by half. Strain the sauce and reserve.

Cut the beans into 5-cm/2-inch lengths. Heat the oil in a wok or frying pan/skillet and stir-fry the onions and beans for 1 minute, add the tofu cakes and stir-fry for a further 1 minute. Add the coconut sauce, sweet chilli/chili sauce and basil leaves and heat through. Serve sprinkled with the sesame seeds.

---

50 g/4 tablespoons unsalted butter

2 leeks, trimmed, split, well washed, then chopped

200 g/8 oz. baking potatoes, chopped

1 garlic clove, crushed

750 g/1½ lb. fresh or frozen peas

1 litre/1 quart Chicken or Vegetable Stock (page 143)

2 tablespoons chopped fresh mint, plus 2 sprigs

sea salt and freshly ground black pepper

crème fraîche or sour cream, to serve

serves 6

PEA + MINT SOUP

Melt the butter in a saucepan, add the leeks, potatoes and garlic, and fry for 10 minutes. Add the peas, stock, mint sprigs and a little salt and pepper and bring to the boil. Cover and simmer for 20 minutes. Discard the mint sprigs.

Transfer the soup to a blender, add the chopped mint, then purée until very smooth. Return to the pan, season to taste and heat through. Serve the soup topped with a spoonful of crème fraîche or sour cream and a generous grinding of black pepper.

We're into fast cooking, so this is a cheat's curry because I have used a ready-made curry paste. Serve with basmati rice.

QUICK VEGETABLE CURRY

3 tablespoons sunflower oil

1 onion, sliced

2 garlic cloves, chopped

3 cm/1 inch fresh ginger, peeled and grated

1 tablespoon hot red curry paste

1 teaspoon ground cinnamon

500 g/1 lb. baking potatoes, cubed

400 g/14 oz. canned chopped tomatoes

300 ml/1¼ cups Vegetable Stock (page 143)

1 tablespoon tomato purée/paste

200 g/8 oz. button mushrooms

200 g/8 oz. frozen peas

25 g/⅓ cup finely ground almonds

2 tablespoons chopped fresh coriander/cilantro

salt and freshly ground black pepper

serves 4

Heat the oil in a saucepan and fry the onion, garlic, ginger, curry paste and cinnamon for 5 minutes. Add the potatoes, tomatoes, stock, tomato purée/paste, salt and pepper. Bring to the boil, cover and simmer gently for 20 minutes.

Halve the mushrooms and add them to the pan with the peas, ground almonds and coriander/cilantro and cook for a further 10 minutes. Taste and adjust the seasoning with salt and pepper, then serve.

Note If you prefer you can use whole blanched almonds and grind them with a mortar and pestle or small blender.

STIR-FRIED SESAME CABBAGE

2 tablespoons peanut oil

1 tablespoon toasted sesame oil

2 garlic cloves, sliced

1 red chilli/chile, seeded and sliced

1 kg/2 lb. Savoy cabbage, finely shredded

1 tablespoon chopped fresh coriander/cilantro

freshly squeezed juice of ½ lemon

50 g/⅓ cup dry-roasted peanuts

2 tablespoons sesame seeds, toasted

sea salt and ground Szechuan pepper

serves 4

Heat the two oils together in a wok or large, deep frying pan/ skillet, add the garlic and chilli/chile and stir-fry over high heat for 30 seconds.

Add the cabbage and stir-fry for a further 2–3 minutes until golden and the cabbage is starting to soften.

Add the coriander/cilantro, lemon juice, peanuts, sesame seeds, salt and pepper, stir well and transfer to a warmed dish. Serve at once.

Basil oil is particularly good sprinkled onto this simple tart, but you can use ordinary olive oil if you prefer. Preheating the baking sheet will make the base of the tart beautifully crisp.

SIMPLE TOMATO + OLIVE TART
with Parmesan

350 g/12 oz. ready-made puff pastry, thawed if frozen

125 g/4 oz. red cherry tomatoes, halved

125 g/4 oz. yellow cherry tomatoes, halved

50 g/½ cup semi-dried or sun-dried tomatoes, halved

50 g/½ cup black olives, such as Niçoise or Kalamata, pitted and halved

2 tablespoons basil oil (below)

25 g/1 oz. freshly grated Parmesan cheese, about ⅓ cup

sea salt and freshly ground black pepper

a handful of rocket/arugula, to serve

basil oil

25 g/1 oz. fresh basil leaves, about 1 cup

150 g/⅔ cup extra virgin olive oil

a pinch of sea salt

2 baking sheets

serves 4

To make the basil oil, blanch the leaves very briefly in boiling water, drain and dry thoroughly with paper towels. Put in a blender, add the oil and salt and blend until very smooth. Pour the oil through a fine seive/strainer, or one lined with cheesecloth. Keep in the refrigerator but return to room temperature before using.

Preheat the oven to 220°C (425°F) Gas 7 and put a baking sheet on the middle shelf.

Roll out the dough on a lightly floured surface to form a rectangle, 25 x 30 cm/10 x 12 inches. Trim the edges and transfer the dough to a second baking sheet. Using the blade of a sharp knife, gently tap the edges several times (this will help the dough rise and the edges separate) and prick all over with a fork.

Put the tomatoes, olives, basil oil, salt and pepper in a bowl and mix lightly. Spoon the mixture over the dough and carefully slide the tart directly onto the preheated baking sheet. Bake for 12–15 minutes until risen and golden.

Remove from the oven and sprinkle with the Parmesan. Cut into quarters and serve hot with a handful of rocket/arugula.

Red lentils are widely used in Indian cooking to make dhaal – a sauce to serve with rice. They are healthy, nutritious and delicious. Serve this dish as part of an Indian meal.

CURRIED RED LENTILS

1 onion, chopped

2 garlic cloves, chopped

3 cm/1 inch fresh ginger, peeled and grated

40 g/4 tablespoons unsalted butter

350 g/12 oz. tomatoes, chopped

1 tablespoon curry powder

1 teaspoon ground turmeric

½ teaspoon ground cinnamon

350 g/12 oz. (about 1¾ cups) red lentils

900 ml/4 cups Vegetable Stock (page 143), or good quality store-bought stock

freshly squeezed juice of ½ lemon

sea salt and freshly ground black pepper

2–3 sprigs of fresh or frozen curry leaves, fried for a few seconds in 2 tablespoons unsalted butter (optional)

serves 6

Put the onion, garlic and ginger in a food processor and blend to form a fairly smooth purée. Heat the butter in a saucepan, add the purée, tomatoes and spices, and fry gently for about 5 minutes.

Add the lentils, stock, lemon juice, salt and pepper, bring to the boil, cover and simmer over low heat for about 20 minutes until the lentils have thickened.

Taste and adjust the seasoning with salt and pepper, then serve topped with a few fried curry leaves, if using.

Although it may sound unusual, chocolate is the secret ingredient of this Mexican-inspired dish. It adds a wonderfully rich, intense flavour to the vegetables. Serve with rice, or the Chilli/Chile Cornbread on page 115.

QUICK VEGETARIAN MOLE

2 tablespoons peanut or safflower oil

1 red onion, chopped

1 large red (bell) pepper, seeded and chopped

2 garlic cloves

2 teaspoons ground coriander

1 teaspoon ground cumin

½ teaspoon ground cinnamon

400 g/1 lb. sweet potatoes, cut into cubes

400 g/1 lb. (about 2 cups) canned chopped tomatoes

400 g/1 lb. (about 2 cups) canned red kidney beans, rinsed and drained

1–2 teaspoons sweet chilli/chili sauce

15–25 g/1 oz. dark chocolate, grated

2 tablespoons chopped fresh coriander/cilantro

sea salt and freshly ground black pepper

serves 4

Heat the oil in a saucepan and fry the onion, pepper, garlic and spices for 5 minutes. Add the sweet potatoes, tomatoes, beans, chilli/chile sauce and 300 ml/1¼ cups water and bring to the boil. Cover and simmer over gentle heat for 30 minutes.

Stir in the chocolate and fresh coriander/cilantro and cook for a final 5 minutes. Taste and adjust the seasoning with salt and pepper, then serve.

STEAMED BABY VEGETABLES
with black bean dressing

1 kg/2 lb. mixed baby vegetables, trimmed, washed and peeled as necessary

BLACK BEAN DRESSING

2 tablespoons canned black beans, drained, rinsed and drained again

1 garlic clove, crushed

1 teaspoon grated fresh ginger

1 tablespoon rice wine vinegar

1 tablespoon light soy sauce

100 g/½ cup peanut oil

serves 6

To make the dressing, put the beans in a bowl, add 3 tablespoons cold water, mash lightly with a fork, then stir in the garlic, ginger, vinegar, soy sauce and peanut oil.

Steam the vegetables over a saucepan of simmering water, starting with the largest and adding the rest depending on size, until the vegetables are tender. Transfer to a large bowl and pass the dressing around in a separate bowl so guests can help themselves.

This recipe is based on a favourite Greek dish – gigantes or 'big beans'.
The Quick Tomato Sauce can be made ahead.

BUTTER/LIMA BEANS
with quick tomato sauce

2 tablespoons extra virgin olive oil

1 onion, chopped

½ teaspoon dried chilli/hot red pepper flakes

800 g/1¾ lb. (about 5 cups) canned butter/lima beans, rinsed and drained

1 recipe Quick Tomato Sauce (page 142)

sea salt and freshly ground black pepper

TO SERVE
toast

freshly grated Parmesan cheese

serves 4

Heat the oil in a saucepan and gently fry the onion and chilli/red pepper flakes for 10 minutes until softened but not golden.

Add the beans, stir once, then add the quick tomato sauce. Bring to the boil, cover with a lid and simmer gently for about 20 minutes. Taste and adjust the seasoning with salt and pepper and serve piled onto toast with a sprinkling of freshly grated Parmesan.

WHITE BEAN SOUP
with olive gremolata

4 tablespoons/¼ cup extra virgin olive oil

1 large onion, chopped

2 garlic cloves, crushed

1 tablespoon chopped fresh sage

500 g/1 lb. baking potatoes, cubed

800 g/1¾ lb. (about 5 cups) canned white beans, drained

1 litre/1 quart Vegetable Stock (page 143)

2 bay leaves

175 g/1 cup pitted black olives, such as Niçoise

grated zest of 1 unwaxed lemon

2 tablespoons chopped fresh parsley

sea salt and freshly ground black pepper

serves 6

Heat the oil in a saucepan and fry the onion, garlic and sage for 5 minutes until golden. Add the potatoes and beans, stir well, then add the stock, bay leaves, salt and pepper.

Bring to the boil, cover and simmer gently for 20 minutes until the potatoes are tender. Transfer half the soup to a blender and blend until smooth. Return to the pan, adjust the seasoning and heat through.

Meanwhile, to make the gremolata, finely chop the olives and mix with lemon zest and parsley. Serve the soup in warm bowls topped with the gremolata.

EGGS + CHEESE

Eggs and dairy products are the victims of a bad press and constantly changing reputations. One minute they're bad for people watching their weight – the next, they're good.

A balanced diet is vital for a healthy body, and eggs and dairy products are excellent sources of protein and calcium which help build strong bones in the young and reduce the chances of osteoporosis in later life. They taste good and are good for you – especially for people who don't eat meat.

The other great thing about egg and cheese dishes is they are usually very quick to make. Take an omelette or scrambled eggs, for instance – ready in minutes. Cheese on toast? A perfect late-night instant snack.

I love dishes like these. I find them comforting and familiar, perhaps because they remind me of the food my mother used to cook for me when I was a kid.

Smoked salmon and baked eggs make the perfect breakfast treat – and take no time at all. In fact, if you're having people over on the weekend for brunch, there can be no quicker, easier or more elegant dish to serve as part of the spread.

BAKED EGGS
with smoked salmon and chives

200 g/8 oz. smoked salmon slices, chopped

1 tablespoon chopped fresh chives

4 eggs

4 tablespoons/¼ cup double/heavy cream

sea salt and freshly ground black pepper

toast, to serve

4 ramekins, 200 ml/1 cup each, well buttered

serves 4

Divide the smoked salmon and chives between the 4 buttered ramekins. Make a small indent in the salmon with the back of a spoon and break an egg in the hollow, sprinkle with a little pepper, and spoon the cream over the top.

Put the ramekins in a roasting pan and half-fill the pan with boiling water. Bake in a preheated oven at 180°C (350°F) Gas 4 for 10–15 minutes until the eggs have just set. Remove from the oven, let cool for a few minutes, then serve with toast.

This recipe serves two because it's not easy to cook more than this quantity at once. Regular or portobello mushrooms are fine, but if you can find wild mushrooms such as girolle or chanterelle, then you are in for a real treat.

SCRAMBLED EGGS
with mushrooms

250 g/8 oz. portobello mushrooms, or mixed wild mushrooms

6 eggs

50 g/4 tablespoons unsalted butter

2 teaspoons chopped fresh thyme leaves

sea salt and freshly ground black pepper

TO SERVE
chopped fresh parsley (optional)

toast

sautéed mushrooms (optional)

serves 2

Wipe the mushrooms with a damp cloth and cut into thick slices. Put the eggs in a bowl, add salt and pepper, and beat until blended.

Melt 40 g/3 tablespoons of the butter in a large frying pan/skillet. As soon as it stops foaming, add the mushrooms, thyme, salt and pepper. Fry over medium heat until lightly browned and the juices are starting to run.

Push the mushrooms to one side of the pan, add the remaining butter, then pour in the beaten eggs, stirring with a fork until almost set.

Gradually stir in the mushrooms from the sides of the pan, cook a moment longer and spoon onto toast. Sprinkle with chopped parsley, if using, and serve with toast.

Perfectly set eggs spiked with the fragrance of mixed fresh herbs makes a great supper dish and I love to dot the frittata with a little ricotta just before the top is grilled/broiled. Cut into small squares for great finger food.

FRITTATA
with fresh herbs and ricotta

6 eggs

a large handful of chopped mixed fresh herbs, such as basil, chervil, chives, marjoram, mint and/or parsley

1 teaspoon celery salt (optional)

2 tablespoons extra virgin olive oil

125 g/4 oz. (about ½ cup) fresh ricotta cheese crumbled into big pieces

sea salt and freshly ground black pepper

serves 4

Put the eggs in a bowl, add the herbs, celery salt, if using, and a good sprinkling of salt and pepper. Beat with a fork.

Preheat the grill/broiler. Heat the oil in a non-stick frying pan/skillet until hot, then add the egg mixture. Cook over medium heat for 5–6 minutes until almost set. Dot the ricotta over the top and cook under a hot grill/broiler until the surface is set and browned.

Let cool slightly, then cut in wedges and serve warm.

BAKED CHÈVRE

4 thick slices of goats' cheese with rind (chèvre), 50 g/2 oz. per serving
extra virgin olive oil, for sprinkling
1 tablespoon chopped fresh thyme
freshly ground black pepper

TO SERVE
4 slices of sourdough bread
1–2 garlic cloves, halved
green salad

a baking sheet, lined with foil

serves 4

Put the slices of chèvre onto the prepared baking sheet, sprinkle with a little oil, dot with thyme leaves and season with pepper. Bake in a preheated oven at 200°C (400°F) Gas 6 for 10–12 minutes until just starting to ooze and run.

Meanwhile, toast the sourdough and rub it with the garlic. When the cheese is ready, spread it onto the toasted, garlicky sourdough and serve with a green salad.

Simple and delicious, this recipe can be served as an appetizer or as a snack with a green salad. Use a creamy goats' cheese with a rind that will soften nicely without melting.

GRILLED/BROILED ASPARAGUS
with goats' cheese and herb oil

500 g/1 lb. asparagus spears
1 tablespoon Thyme Oil (page 140), plus extra to serve
125 g/4 oz. goats' cheese, sliced
sea salt and freshly ground black pepper
baguette, to serve

serves 4

Preheat the grill/broiler. Trim the asparagus spears and rub or brush with a little of the Thyme Oil, sprinkle with salt and pepper, and cook under a hot grill/broiler for 4–5 minutes, turning half-way through until charred and tender.

Arrange on plates and top each one with a slice of the cheese, return to the grill/broiler very briefly until the cheese is softened but not browned. Sprinkle with more Thyme Oil and serve with crusty bread.

My favourite thing when I get back late from the movies or a show – quick, delicious and washing-up-free. It tastes great with almost any chutney or relish. Be ready to provide seconds.

CHEESE ON TOAST

2 thick slices of white bread

125 g/4 oz. cheese, such as Cheddar, a soft creamy goats' cheese or Brie

a few drops of Worcestershire sauce (optional)

pickles, relish, or chutney, to serve

serves 2

Toast the bread under the grill/broiler on one side only. Grate the cheese onto the untoasted side of the bread (if using very soft cheese, slice it instead). Add a few drops of Worcestershire sauce, if using and grill/broil for 2–3 minutes until melted and bubbling.

Serve on a platter with the bottle of pickles, relish or chutney and a spoon so that guests can help themselves.

Make this dish only when top-quality fresh figs are in season. Otherwise use peaches, nectarines or melon wedges.

FIGS WITH MARINATED FETA

1 garlic clove, crushed

1 red chilli/chile, seeded and chopped

grated zest of 1 unwaxed lemon

½ teaspoon ground cumin

1 tablespoon chopped fresh mint

6 tablespoons/⅓ cup extra virgin olive oil

250 g/8 oz. feta cheese, crumbled

4–6 large ripe figs

4 slices toasted sourdough bread

cracked black pepper

Reduced Balsamic Vinegar, to serve (page 141)

serves 4

Put the garlic, chilli/chile, lemon zest, cumin, mint and oil in a bowl, add the feta and toss gently. Set aside to marinate for at least 30 minutes (this can be done the night before).

Slice the figs in half and serve on the toasted bread with the feta and marinade juices, then serve sprinkled with a little Reduced Balsamic Vinegar.

Served warm, these soufflés are a favourite of mine because I don't have to panic getting them to the table before they sink! Make sure you butter the ramekin dishes very well so that you can get the soufflés out.

WARM GOATS' CHEESE SOUFFLES

25 g/2 tablespoons unsalted butter

2 tablespoons plain/all-purpose flour

250 ml/1 cup milk

100 g/4 oz. soft goats' cheese

3 eggs, separated

2 tablespoons chopped fresh mixed herbs, such as basil, chives, mint and tarragon

sea salt and freshly ground black pepper

rocket/arugula salad, to serve

6 ramekins, 200 ml/1 cup each, well buttered

serves 6

Melt the butter in a saucepan, add the flour, and cook over low heat for 30 seconds. Remove the pan from the heat and gradually stir in the milk until smooth. Return to the heat and stir constantly until the mixture thickens. Cook for 1 minute.

Cool slightly and beat in the cheese, egg yolks, herbs, salt and pepper. Put the egg whites in a bowl and beat until soft peaks form. Fold the egg whites into the cheese mixture.

Spoon the mixture into the ramekins and bake in a preheated oven 200°C (400°F) Gas 6 for 15–18 minutes until risen and golden on top. Remove from the oven and let cool for about 15 minutes.

Using a spatula, work round the edges of the soufflés and turn them out onto plates. Serve with rocket/arugula salad.

FISH + SEAFOOD

Since moving to Australia, I have learned a great deal about the freshness of seafood, something that is unfortunately not always available in other countries.

However, top-quality seafood can be found, and it is usually just a case of seeking out a good supplier. Supermarkets are improving all the time and will only continue to do so if you, the customer, demand quality.

Don't be afraid to talk to your fishmongers, ask them questions – most are only too glad to share their knowledge.

When shopping for shellfish, avoid any that are sitting in water, and when buying fish, look for bright eyes and shiny skin. They should smell of the sea (not at all fishy).

Simplicity is the name of the game when you're cooking seafood. Let the flavours speak for themselves by serving it quickly cooked and simply dressed – perhaps just with a drizzle of oil and fragrant chopped herbs or a pat of spiced butter.

Prawns/shrimp make the fastest, freshest, most impressive dish you can imagine. If you can't find uncooked prawns/shrimp, use precooked ones – just sprinkle them with the chilli/chili oil and lemon juice and serve with the cool and refreshing pesto. Now, how complicated can that be!

PRAWNS/SHRIMP WITH CHILLI OIL
and pistachio and mint Pesto

24 large uncooked prawns/shrimp, shelled and deveined

4 tablespoons/¼ cup Chilli/Chili Oil (page 140)

freshly squeezed juice of 1 lemon

pistachio and mint pesto

50 g/2 oz. (about ⅓ cup) shelled pistachios

a bunch of mint

1 garlic clove, crushed

2 spring onions/scallions, chopped

125 g/½ cup extra virgin olive oil

1 tablespoon white wine vinegar

sea salt and freshly ground black pepper

TO SERVE
1 lemon, cut into wedges

crusty bread

serves 4

To make the pesto, put the pistachios, mint, garlic and spring onions/scallions in a food processor and grind coarsely. Add the oil and purée until fairly smooth and green. Stir in the vinegar and season to taste. Set aside while you prepare the prawns/shrimp, or store in the refrigerator for up to 5 days.

Put the prawns/shrimp in a shallow dish and sprinkle with the Chilli/Chili Oil, salt and pepper. Cover and let marinate for at least 30 minutes or longer, if possible.

When ready to serve, thread the prawns/shrimp onto skewers and cook on a preheated barbecue or stove-top grill pan, or under a hot grill/broiler, for about 2 minutes on each side until charred and tender – the flesh should be just opaque. Do not overcook or the prawns/shrimp will be tough.

Put on separate plates or a large platter, sprinkle with fresh lemon juice and serve with the pesto and crusty bread to mop up the juices.

Try to find small vongole clams – I think they are sweeter and more tender than the larger varieties. This recipe will serve four as an appetizer, but you can serve it with other Asian dishes plus rice and noodles for an impressive banquet.

DRUNKEN CLAMS

2 kg/4 lb. fresh clams, well scrubbed

150 g/⅔ cup Fish or Vegetable Stock (page 143)

100 ml/½ cup Shaohsing (sweetened Chinese rice wine) or sweet sherry

4 garlic cloves, sliced

3 cm/1 inch fresh ginger, peeled and sliced

6 spring onions/scallions, sliced

1 red chilli/chile, seeded and sliced

Szechuan pepper or black pepper

serves 4

Tap each clam lightly on the work surface and discard any that won't close. Put the clams in a saucepan, add the stock, rice wine, garlic, ginger, spring onions/scallions and chilli/chile. Grind Szechuan pepper over the top and bring to the boil. Cover with a lid and let steam for 3–4 minutes until all the shells have opened.

Discard any unopened clams and transfer the rest to warmed bowls. Pour the stock through a fine sieve/strainer, pour over the clams, then serve.

A simple dish with lovely flavours – when you serve lobster, the effect is instantly luxurious and 'special occasion'. Who would ever know this dish was so simple to prepare? Slice the fennel as finely as possible, using a mandoline if you have one. If not, it's worthwhile investing in one so you can cut vegetables very thinly into slices or matchsticks. Inexpensive, but effective, plastic Japanese mandolines are available from kitchen stores.

LOBSTER AND FENNEL SALAD

1 large bulb of fennel

freshly squeezed juice of ½ lemon

4 tablespoons/¼ cup extra virgin olive oil

4 small cooked lobsters, about 500 g/1 lb. each, or 2 large ones

1 recipe Mayonnaise (page 142)

sea salt and freshly ground black pepper

serves 4

Trim off and discard the tough outer layer of fennel, then chop and reserve the fronds. Cut the bulb in half, then cut crossways into very thin slices. Put in a bowl, add the lemon juice, oil, fennel fronds, salt and pepper, toss well, then marinate for 15 minutes.

Cut the lobsters in half and lift the tail flesh out of the shell. Crack the claws with a small hammer or crab crackers and carefully remove all the meat.

Put a layer of shaved fennel salad on each plate, top with the lobster, and serve with a spoonful of mayonnaise.

The squid will curl up as they cook, so I use a pair of tongs to open them out again and press flat. You could also put a heatproof plate on top to keep them that way. Take care not to overcook squid or it will be tough.

SEARED SQUID
with lemon and coriander/cilantro dressing

4 medium squid, cleaned, about 750 g/1½ lb.

1 tablespoon extra virgin olive oil

sea salt and freshly ground black pepper

baby spinach leaves, to serve

LEMON AND CORIANDER/
CILANTRO DRESSING

5 tablespoons/⅓ cup peanut oil

1 tablespoon toasted sesame oil

freshly squeezed juice of 1 lemon

2 tablespoons sweet soy sauce, (Indonesian ketchap manis), or regular soy sauce with ½ teaspoon sugar added

2 tablespoons chopped fresh coriander/cilantro

1 garlic clove, crushed

serves 4

To make the dressing, put the ingredients in a screw-top bottle, shake well and use as required. If storing in the refrigerator, omit the coriander/cilantro and add just before use.

Cut the squid bodies in half and open out flat. Brush with the olive oil and season with salt and pepper.

Heat a stove-top grill pan for 5 minutes until very hot. Add the squid bodies and tentacles and cook for 1 minute on each side until charred and tender. Transfer to a board and cut the squid into thick slices.

Put the dressing in a bowl, add the squid and toss well. Serve with a few baby spinach leaves and extra black pepper.

Note Squid is very easy to clean. Pull out the tentacles (the insides should come with them). Cut off the tentacles and discard the insides. Rinse out the bodies, pulling out the stiff transparent quill, like a little wand of plastic. Use the bodies and tentacles. That's it.

Scallops, with their sweet flesh and subtle hint of the sea, are a real treat. Truffle oil, though expensive, is used sparingly and transforms this dish into something special. If you don't have any truffle oil, use either Thyme Oil (page 140) or Fragrant Garlic Oil (page 21).

SEARED SCALLOPS
with crushed potatoes

12 large sea scallops
1 tablespoon extra virgin olive oil
sea salt and freshly ground black
  pepper

CRUSHED POTATOES
1 lb. new potatoes, peeled
1 tablespoon extra virgin olive oil
¼ cup pitted black olives, chopped
1 tablespoon chopped
fresh flat-leaf parsley
a few drops of truffle oil (optional)
sea salt and freshly ground black
  pepper

serves 4

Cook the potatoes in a saucepan of lightly salted, boiling water until just tender. Drain well and return to the pan. Lightly crush them with a fork leaving them still a little chunky. Add the olive oil, olives, parsley, and a few drops of truffle oil, if using. Season with salt and pepper and stir well.

Put the scallops in a bowl, add the olive oil, salt and pepper. Sear the scallops on a preheated stove-top grill pan for 1 minute on each side (don't overcook or they will be tough). Remove to a plate and let them rest briefly.

Put a pile of crushed potatoes onto each plate, put the scallops on top, and sprinkle with a few extra drops of truffle oil, if using.

Peppery radish and fresh mint yogurt tempers the heat from the spice-coated fish, though if you don't like very spicy food, you could leave out the chilli/chili powder and rely on the freshly ground black pepper and crunchy radishes alone. Serve crusty bread on the side to mop up the juices.

BLACKENED MONKFISH
with radish and mint yogurt

4 fillets monkfish or cod, 200 g/8 oz. each, skinned

50 g/4 tablespoons unsalted butter

1 tablespoon peanut oil

200 g/1 cup plain yogurt

4 radishes, cut into matchstick strips, plus extra to serve

½ cucumber, peeled, seeded, and cut into matchstick strips

1 tablespoon chopped fresh mint

1 garlic clove, crushed

sea salt and freshly ground black pepper

SPICE MIX
2 tablespoons chopped fresh
thyme leaves

1 tablespoon ground cumin

1 tablespoon sea salt

2 teaspoons ground allspice

2 teaspoons crushed black pepper

½ teaspoon chilli/chili powder

serves 4

Mix all the spice mix ingredients together and sprinkle on a plate. Roll the fish in the spice mix until well coated.

Melt the butter and oil in a nonstick frying pan/skillet, then as soon as it stops foaming, add the fish. Fry over medium heat for 4 minutes on each side, until browned all over. Transfer to a warm oven and let rest for 5 minutes.

Put the yogurt in a bowl, add the radishes, cucumber, mint, garlic, salt and pepper, and stir well. Serve with the browned fish.

Salmon is always better a little pink in the middle. If you cook fish too long, it will become dry and tasteless. To avoid this, sear it on the skin side first at a fairly high heat. The skin will caramelize a little, then when you turn it over you need only brown the flesh side for a short time. Very fast and fresh!

SEARED SALMON
with cucumber pickle

4 salmon fillets, 200 g/8 oz. each
1 tablespoon toasted sesame oil
sea salt and crushed Szechuan
   pepper or black pepper
green salad, to serve

CUCUMBER PICKLE
1 cucumber, about 20 cm/8 inches
   long
2 teaspoons salt
60 ml/¼ cup rice vinegar
3 tablespoons sugar
1 red chilli/chile, seeded and sliced
3 cm/1 inch fresh ginger, peeled
   and grated

serves 4

To make the cucumber pickle, cut the cucumber in half lengthways, scoop out and discard the seeds, and cut the flesh into 1 cm/½-inch slices. Put the salt, rice vinegar, sugar, chilli/chile and ginger in a bowl, add 4 tablespoons/¼ cup water and mix well. Pour over the cucumber and set aside to marinate.

Brush the salmon fillets with the sesame oil and season with salt and crushed Szechuan pepper. Put the fillets skin side down onto a preheated stove-top grill pan and cook for 4 minutes. Turn the salmon over and cook for a further 1 minute.

Remove from the pan, let rest for a few moments, then serve with the cucumber pickle and a crisp green salad.

I love to serve this dish whenever I see some really fresh swordfish at the market. It is easy to overcook swordfish, which will become tough, so follow the timings below and err on the side of caution – you can always put the fish back on the heat for a moment or two longer if necessary.

SEARED SWORDFISH
with new potatoes, beans and olives

4 swordfish steaks, 200 g/8 oz. each

7 tablespoons/½ cup extra virgin olive oil

2 tablespoons freshly squeezed lemon juice

½ teaspoon caster/granulated sugar

1 tablespoon chopped fresh chives

500 g/1 lb, new potatoes, halved if large

200 g/8 oz. green/string beans, trimmed

50 g/2 oz. black olives, such as Niçoise or Kalamata, pitted and chopped, about ½ cup

sea salt and freshly ground black pepper

Reduced Balsamic Vinegar (page 141), to serve

serves 4

Brush the swordfish steaks with 1 tablespoon of the oil, season with salt and pepper and set aside.

To make the dressing, put the remaining oil in a bowl, add the lemon juice, sugar, chives, salt and pepper then beat well and set aside.

Cook the potatoes in a saucepan of lightly salted boiling water for 10 minutes, add the beans and cook for a further 3–4 minutes or until the potatoes and beans are just tender. Drain well, add the olives and half the dressing and toss well.

Cook the swordfish steaks on a preheated outdoor grill or stove-top grill pan for about 1½ minutes on each side. Let rest in a warm oven for 5 minutes, then serve with the warm potato and bean salad, sprinkled with the remaining dressing and balsamic vinegar.

POULTRY + MEAT

I grew up on a farm where we kept hens that were allowed to feed on the grain left behind after the corn had been harvested. They gorged themselves happily on such wonderful food that the benefits to both them and us were obvious to everyone. Now I always buy organic, free-range chicken. It is more expensive, but worth every penny.

For many people, duck is probably seen as a bit of a luxury, because it is expensive and sometimes difficult to find. However, it's ideal for cooks short of time, because the breasts cook very quickly. They are sold in many supermarkets, or you can buy a whole duck from the butchers and ask them to cut it into pieces for you (freeze the rest for another time).

When shopping for meat, look for flesh with a good deep colour and a layer of fat around it which will keep it moist during cooking. Fat should be creamy in colour and almost matt in appearance.

Remember, whatever meat you are cooking, it will need a little time to rest before eating, this lets the meat relax so it is more tender.

Jerk seasoning is Jamaica's popular spice mix, used to spark up meat, poultry and fish, especially the delicious barbecued offerings sold at the roadside jerk huts so beloved of tourists and locals alike. The seasoning is a combination of allspice, cinnamon, chilli/chili, nutmeg, thyme and sugar and is available in powder or paste form from larger supermarkets and specialty food stores.*

JERK CHICKEN WINGS
with avocado salsa

12 chicken wings

2 tablespoons extra virgin olive oil

1 tablespoon jerk seasoning powder or 2 tablespoons paste

freshly squeezed juice of ½ lemon

1 teaspoon sea salt

AVOCADO SALSA

1 large ripe avocado

2 ripe tomatoes, peeled, seeded and chopped

1 garlic clove, crushed

1 small red chilli/chile, seeded and chopped

freshly squeezed juice of ½ lemon

2 tablespoons chopped fresh coriander/cilantro

1 tablespoon extra virgin olive oil

sea salt and freshly ground black pepper

serves 4

Put the chicken wings in a ceramic dish. Mix the oil, jerk seasoning, lemon juice and salt in a bowl, pour over the wings and stir well to coat. Let marinate overnight.

The next day cook the wings either on a preheated barbecue or under a hot grill/broiler for 5–6 minutes on each side, basting occasionally with any remaining marinade until charred and tender.

Meanwhile, to make the salsa, put all the ingredients in a bowl, mix well and season to taste. Serve the wings with the salsa.

Note If you don't have any jerk seasoning on hand, try another spice mix or spice paste instead. Just remember, jerk is very fiery indeed, so you need a spicy one.

Chinese five-spice powder is a ready-made spice mix used widely in Asian cooking. It is made up of cassia bark (similar to cinnamon), cloves, fennel, star anise and Szechuan pepper.

ROAST FIVE-SPICE CHICKEN
with Ginger Bok Choy

4 chicken quarters (breasts or legs)

2 tablespoons sunflower oil

1 teaspoon Chinese five-spice powder

3 cm/1 inch fresh ginger, peeled and grated

½ teaspoon salt

3 tablespoons honey

1½ tablespoons dark soy sauce

GINGER BOK CHOY

3 tablespoons soy sauce

1 tablespoon sweet chilli/chili sauce

2 tablespoons sunflower oil

2 teaspoons sesame oil

3 cm/1 inch fresh ginger, peeled and finely sliced into matchstick strips

8 small bok choy, halved, well washed, and patted dry with paper towels

serves 4

Wash and dry the chicken pieces and put in a roasting pan.

Put the oil, five-spice powder, ginger and salt in a bowl, mix well, then brush all over the chicken. Roast in a preheated oven at 200°C (400°F) Gas 6 for 25 minutes.

Put the honey and soy sauce in a small saucepan and heat until the honey has melted. Stir well, then brush all over the chicken to form a glaze. Return to the oven and roast for a further 10 minutes until the skin is crisp and golden.

To prepare the bok choy, put the soy sauce, chilli/chili sauce, and 4 tablespoons/¼ cup water in a bowl and mix well.

Heat the two oils in a wok or large frying pan/skillet, add the ginger and stir-fry for 30 seconds. Add the bok choy and continue to stir-fry for a further 2 minutes. Add the soy sauce mixture, cover and simmer gently for 2 minutes, then serve with the chicken.

A great supper dish – simple and quick. Serve it with a green salad, or with this more substantial dish of beans and leeks, which is also very good served with lamb. The Mustard and Tarragon Butter is very versatile and is delicious served with fish such as salmon.

PAN-FRIED CHICKEN
with Creamy beans and leeks

4 chicken boneless breasts

25 g/2 tablespoons unsalted butter

1 tablespoon extra virgin olive oil

1 recipe Mustard and Tarragon Butter (page 140)

sea salt and freshly ground black pepper

watercress salad, to serve

CREAMY FLAGEOLET/CANNELLINI BEANS WITH LEEKS

4 tablespoons unsalted butter

2 leeks, finely chopped

1 garlic clove, crushed

2 teaspoons chopped fresh rosemary

2 cans flageolet/cannellini beans, 400 g/15 oz. each, drained, rinsed and drained again

300 ml/1¼ cups Vegetable Stock (page 143)

4 tablespoons/¼ cup double/heavy cream

sea salt and freshly ground black pepper

serves 4

To cook the beans and leeks, melt the butter in a saucepan, add the leeks, garlic, and rosemary, and fry gently for 5 minutes until softened but not golden.

Add the beans, stir once, then pour in the stock. Bring to the boil, cover, and simmer for 15 minutes. Remove the lid, stir in the cream, and add salt and pepper to taste. Simmer, uncovered, for a further 5 minutes until the sauce has thickened. Set aside while you prepare the chicken.

Season the chicken with salt and pepper. Heat the butter and oil in a frying pan/skillet and as soon as the butter stops foaming, cook the chicken skin side down for 4 minutes. Turn it over and cook for a further 4 minutes.

Top each breast with a couple of slices of the Mustard and Tarragon Butter and let rest for 2–3 minutes in a warm oven. Serve with the beans and a simple watercress salad.

These mini chickens can be roasted in about 40 minutes. To make sure they are cooked through, push a skewer into the leg meat right down to the bone – if the juices run clear, the bird is cooked. If not, return to the oven for a little longer.

GARLIC-ROASTED BIRDS

2 whole heads of garlic, cloves separated but unpeeled

2 large poussins/Cornish hens

½ lemon

4 sprigs of thyme

4 tablespoons unsalted butter, softened

100 ml/½ cup white wine

300 ml/1¼ cups Chicken Stock (page 143)

1 tablespoon plain/all-purpose flour

sea salt and freshly ground black pepper

serves 4

Boil the garlic cloves in a saucepan of lightly salted water for 15 minutes, drain and pat dry (this can be done ahead of time).

Meanwhile, rub the birds all over with the cut lemon. Chop the lemon into small chunks and put them and the thyme in the body cavities. Season well with salt and pepper and rub the birds all over with 40 g/3 tablespoons of the butter.

Put 1 garlic clove in each bird, then put the rest in a large roasting pan. Sit the birds on top and roast in a preheated oven at 200°C (400°F) Gas 6 for 40 minutes.

Transfer the birds and garlic cloves to a large plate, wrap loosely in foil, and let rest for 10 minutes.

Meanwhile, to make a gravy, spoon off any excess fat from the roasting pan. Add the wine, bring to the boil and scrape any sediments into the wine. Boil until reduced by two-thirds. Add the stock and boil for 5 minutes, or until reduced by half. Put the remaining butter and the flour in a bowl and beat until smooth. Gradually beat into the gravy, stirring, over gentle heat until thickened. Serve the birds with the garlic and gravy.

Duck breasts make a quick and easy dish. Cook them in a stove-top grill pan or heavy frying pan/skillet. The skin will turn very black and crispy from the sugar, and the rich flesh is balanced perfectly by the sweetness of spiced plums.

DUCK WITH SPICED PLUMS

4 duck breasts, 200 g/8 oz. each

1 tablespoon honey

1 tablespoon dark soy sauce

25 ml/2 tablespoons rice wine vinegar

25 g/2 tablespoons palm sugar or soft brown sugar*

¼ teaspoon ground cinnamon

4 plums, halved and pitted

sea salt and freshly ground black pepper

serves 4

Using a sharp knife, cut several slashes in the duck skin. Rub the skin with salt and pepper. Put the honey and soy sauce in a shallow dish, stir well, add the duck breasts and let marinate for at least 15 minutes.

Put the vinegar, sugar, cinnamon and 2 tablespoons water in a saucepan and heat until the sugar dissolves. Bring to the boil, add the plums and simmer gently for 8–10 minutes until the plums have softened. Let cool.

Meanwhile, heat a stove-top grill pan or heavy frying pan/skillet until hot, add the duck skin side down, and cook over medium heat for 5 minutes. Turn and cook for a further 4–5 minutes, then remove from the heat and let rest in a low oven for 5 minutes.

Slice the duck crossways and serve with the plums and a little of the spiced juice.

Note Palm sugar and other Asian ingredients are available in Chinese stores. If unavailable, use brown or regular sugar.

A simple dish – the Japanese ingredients such as pickled ginger and seven-spice are available in any supermarket selling sushi ingredients. However, go sparingly with the seven-spice pepper – it's a hot little number.

JAPANESE BEEF TATAKI

250 g/8 oz. beef fillet/tenderloin
1 tablespoon sunflower oil
Japanese seven-spice pepper
(shichimi togarashi)
5-cm/2-inch piece of daikon (mooli or
   white radish), peeled and grated
Japanese pickled ginger

DIPPING SAUCE
4 tablespoons/¼ cup Japanese soy
   sauce (shoyu)
4 teaspoons sake or mirin (sweetened
   Japanese rice wine)

serves 4

Brush the meat with the oil and dust very lightly with the seven-spice pepper. Heat a heavy frying pan/skillet for 5 minutes until very hot, then add the beef and sear on all sides for 2–3 minutes until evenly browned. Remove from the pan and let cool.

Put the dipping sauce ingredients in a bowl, add 4 tablespoons/¼ cup water, mix well, then divide between 4 small dipping bowls.

Using a very sharp knife, slice the beef thinly and arrange on plates with a little mound of daikon and ginger on each one. Serve with the dipping sauce.

It's important to rest meat for a short time before serving to let it relax and the juices from the steak mingle with the butter. You can serve it with any kind of flavoured butter – make up several different kinds, roll them into logs, wrap them in foil and store them in the freezer to use whenever you need a fast and flavourful addition to a dish. They are good with beef, fish, poultry and even vegetables.

PAN-FRIED STEAK
with horseradish butter

4 fillet/rib-eye steaks, about 200 g/
   8 oz. each
2 tablespoons extra virgin olive oil
sea salt and freshly ground black
   pepper
horseradish and chive butter
125 g/1¼ sticks unsalted butter,
   softened
1½ tablespoons grated fresh
   horseradish
1 tablespoon chopped fresh chives

TO SERVE (OPTIONAL)
sautéed potatoes
green salad

serves 4

To make the horseradish and chive butter, put the butter, horseradish and chives in a bowl and beat well. Season to taste with salt and pepper. Form into a log, wrap in foil and chill for about 30 minutes.

Season the steaks with salt and pepper. Heat the oil in a frying pan/skillet until very hot and fry the steaks over medium-high heat for 3 minutes on each side for rare, or a little longer for medium.

Top each steak with 2 slices of the horseradish butter and set aside to rest in a warm oven for 5 minutes, then serve with sautéed potatoes and salad.

The spices and flavourings used in this recipe are typical of North African cooking, and all over the region, pitta/pita bread is stuffed with grilled meat, salad and yogurt. Use other minced/ground meats if you prefer.

LAMB IN PITTA BREAD

2 teaspoons coriander seeds

1 teaspoon cumin seeds

2 tablespoons extra virgin olive oil

1 onion, finely chopped

2 garlic cloves, crushed

1 teaspoon ground cinnamon

¼–½ teaspoon cayenne pepper

300 g/10 oz. minced/ground lamb

a pinch of sea salt

2 tablespoons chopped fresh coriander/cilantro

4 pitta/pita bread pockets

a few salad leaves, such as cos/romaine lettuce and watercress

plain yogurt or tahini sauce

1 tablespoon white sesame seeds, toasted in a dry frying pan/skillet

serves 4

Put the coriander and cumin seeds in a small frying pan/skillet without oil and fry until they start to brown and release their aroma. Let cool slightly, then grind to powder in a spice grinder (use a clean coffee grinder) or using a mortar and pestle.

Heat the oil in a frying pan/skillet, add the onion, garlic and ground spices, and fry gently for 5 minutes until softened but not golden. Increase the heat, add the lamb and the pinch of salt, and stir-fry for 5–8 minutes until well browned. Stir in the fresh coriander/cilantro.

Meanwhile, lightly toast the pitta/pita bread and cut a long slit in the side of each one. Carefully fill with a few salad leaves, add the ground lamb mixture, a spoonful of yogurt or tahini and sprinkle with sesame seeds. Serve hot.

Pork can easily become dry. The solution is not to cook it at too high a heat, and in this recipe the sage and Parma ham or prosciutto wrapping help to keep it moist. They have the added advantage of lending more flavour as well. Add the fillets to the pan seam side down so that the ham doesn't unwrap during cooking.

PARMA-WRAPPED PORK
with spinach and lentil salad

2 pork fillets/tenderloins, 350 g/12 oz. each

8 thin slices Parma Ham or prosciutto

12 large sage leaves, plus
   1 tablespoon chopped fresh sage

3 tablespoons extra virgin olive oil

4 shallots, finely chopped

1 garlic clove, crushed

2 cans lentils, 400 g/15 oz. each, drained

100 ml/½ cup Chicken Stock
   (page 143)

freshly squeezed juice of ½ lemon

125 g/4 oz. baby spinach leaves

sea salt and freshly ground black pepper

serves 4

Cut the pork fillets/tenderloins in half crossways to make 4 servings. Season with salt and pepper. Put 2 slices of Parma Ham or prosciutto on a work surface, overlapping them slightly. Add 3 of the sage leaves in a line down the middle. Top with a pork fillet and roll up, keeping the join underneath. Repeat with the remaining fillets.

Heat half the oil in a frying pan/skillet, add the pork fillets seam side down and fry over medium heat for about 12–15 minutes, turning frequently until evenly browned. Transfer to a warm oven and let rest for 5 minutes.

Meanwhile, add the remaining oil to the pan, add the shallots, garlic and the 1 tablespoon chopped sage and fry for 3 minutes until softened but not golden.

Add the lentils, chicken stock and lemon juice and heat through for 2–3 minutes. Stir in the spinach, cook until just wilted and serve with the pork.

The credit for this recipe goes to my mother, who once served leftover fruit compote (the remains of a crazy day's jam/jelly making) with pork chops. It was delicious. Fry the meat over medium heat so you don't burn the wonderful pan juices, which you then pour over the finished dish.

PORK STEAKS
with apple and blackberry compote

4 large pork steaks, about 250 g/8 oz. each
50 g/4 tablespoons unsalted butter
12 large sage leaves
sea salt and freshly ground black pepper

APPLE AND BLACKBERRY COMPOTE
250 g/8 oz. baking apples, cored and cut into thin wedges
75 g/⅔ cup blackberries
2 tablespoons sugar
freshly squeezed juice of ½ lemon
3 juniper berries

serves 4

To make the sauce, put the apples, blackberries, sugar, lemon juice, juniper berries and 2 tablespoons water in a saucepan. Cover and cook gently until the fruits have softened. Remove the lid and simmer until the juices have evaporated. Remove from the heat, but keep the mixture warm.

Season the chops with salt and pepper. Melt the butter in a large frying pan/skillet and, as soon as it stops foaming, add the pork. Cook over medium heat for 3–4 minutes on each side until browned and cooked through.

Let rest in a warm oven for 5 minutes. Meanwhile add the sage leaves to the same pan and fry for a few seconds until crispy. Serve the steaks topped with a spoonful of the compote, the sage leaves and pan juices.

PASTA, RICE + NOODLES

Pasta, rice and noodles play a major role in cuisines around the world – from Asia and India to the Mediterranean and the Middle East, and the rest of the world has adopted them with open arms.

There are many different varieties of rice used in these countries, including basmati in India and Pakistan, sticky rice and black rice in Southeast Asia, the huge number of different rices in Japan, and of course the short-grain Italian rice used in risotto. In most rice-producing countries rice is served at every meal, much as we serve bread in the West. Well, not always!

Noodles are used throughout Asia much as pasta is served in the Mediterranean, and form the basis of many dishes.

These staples provide our main source of carbohydrate and I love them as much for their versatility as their taste. You could cook pasta, noodle and rice dishes every day of the week without ever feeling bored.

Most Asian noodle dishes take just a matter of minutes to cook – in fact, noodles made of rice flour or mung bean starch are ready almost instantly. Wheat-based noodles take the most time to cook – but even then, only about the same as regular dried pasta.

GINGERED CHICKEN NOODLES

2 tablespoons rice wine, such as Chinese Shaohsing or Japanese mirin

2 teaspoons cornstarch

350 g/12 oz. skinless chicken breasts

175 g/7 oz. Chinese dried egg noodles

3 tablespoons peanut or sunflower oil

3 cm/1 inch fresh ginger, peeled and thinly sliced

125 g/4 oz. mangetout/snowpeas, finely sliced

4 tablespoons/¼ cup chopped fresh garlic chives or chives

125 g/4 oz. (about 1 cup) cashews, toasted in a dry frying pan/skillet, then chopped

SAUCE
100 ml/½ cup Chicken Stock (page 143)

2 tablespoons dark soy sauce

1 tablespoon freshly squeezed lemon juice

1 tablespoon toasted sesame oil

2 teaspoons light brown sugar

serves 4

Put the rice wine and cornstarch in a bowl and mix well. Cut the chicken into small chunks, add to the bowl, stir well and set aside to marinate while you prepare the remaining ingredients.

Soak the noodles according to the instructions on the package, then drain and shake dry.

Put all the sauce ingredients in a small bowl and mix well.

Drain the chicken. Heat 1½ tablespoons of the oil in a wok or large frying pan/skillet, then add the chicken and stir-fry for 2 minutes until golden. Remove to a plate and wipe the pan clean. Add the remaining 1½ tablespoons oil, ginger and mangetout/snowpeas and stir-fry for 1 minute. Return the chicken to the pan, then add the noodles and sauce. Heat through for 2 minutes.

Add the garlic chives and cashews, stir well and serve.

The instant dashi stock and miso soup stock used in Japanese cooking are available from some larger supermarkets or Asian food stores. Alternatively, use good-quality fresh fish stock.

UDON NOODLES
with seven-spice salmon

250 g/8 oz. dried udon noodles

1.5 litres/1½ quarts dashi or miso stock (see recipe introduction)

50 ml/¼ cup mirin (sweetened Japanese rice wine) or dry sherry

50 ml/¼ cup dark soy sauce

100 g/4 oz. firm tofu, cut into cubes

6 spring onions/scallions, trimmed and sliced

a few strands of dried wakame seaweed

4 salmon fillets, 200 g/8 oz. each

1 tablespoon sunflower or peanut oil

Japanese seven-spice pepper (shichimi togarashi), (see recipe introduction, page 79)

serves 4

To cook the noodles, plunge them into a saucepan of boiling water, return to the boil and simmer for 4 minutes until tender. Drain and refresh under cold water, drain again and pat dry with paper towels.

Put the dashi or miso stock in a saucepan, add the mirin, soy sauce, tofu, spring onions/scallions and wakame, and bring to the boil.

Brush the salmon with the oil and dust with a little seven-spice powder. Put the fillets skin side down on a preheated stove-top grill pan for 4 minutes, then turn and cook for a further 1 minute.

Divide the noodles between 4 deep warmed soup bowls, then add the stock, tofu and vegetables. Put the salmon on top and serve.

'Tartare' means uncooked and, to serve fish this way, you must use very fresh, sashimi-grade tuna. If you prefer your tuna cooked, sear it on a preheated stove-top grill pan for 1 minute on each side or until cooked to your liking. However, I do urge you to try it tartare – as the Japanese know, it is delicious.

CHILLI + TUNA TARTARE PASTA

350 g/12 oz. dried fusilli or other pasta

6 tablespoons/⅓ cup extra virgin olive oil

4 garlic cloves, sliced

1–2 dried red chillies/chiles, seeded and chopped

grated zest and juice of 1 unwaxed lemon

1 tablespoon chopped fresh thyme leaves

500 g/1 lb. tuna steak, chopped

a handful of fresh basil leaves

sea salt and freshly ground black pepper

serves 4

Cook the pasta according to the instructions on the package.

Meanwhile, heat the oil in a frying pan/skillet, add the garlic and fry gently for 2 minutes until lightly golden. Add the chilli/chile, lemon zest and thyme and fry for a further 1 minute.

Drain the pasta, reserving 4 tablespoons/¼ cup of the cooking liquid and return both to the pan. Stir in the hot garlic oil mixture, the lemon juice, the raw tuna, basil leaves, salt and pepper and a little extra olive oil. Serve at once.

This sauce is best made as soon as the new season's tomatoes arrive in the stores, especially the vine-ripened varieties that we see more and more. If you don't cook with gas, then simply plunge the tomatoes in boiling water for 1 minute, drain, refresh and peel off the skin.

PASTA WITH FRESH TOMATO

1 kg/2 lb. ripe tomatoes

6 tablespoons/⅓ cup extra virgin olive oil

2 fresh red chillies/chiles, seeded and chopped

2 garlic cloves, crushed

a bunch of fresh basil, chopped

1 teaspoon caster/granulated sugar

350 g/12 oz. dried spaghetti

sea salt and freshly ground black pepper

freshly grated pecorino or Parmesan cheese, to serve

serves 4

Holding each tomato with tongs or a skewer, char them over a gas flame until the skins blister and start to shrivel. Peel off the skins, chop the flesh and put in a bowl. Add the oil, chillies/chiles, garlic, basil, sugar, salt and pepper and leave to infuse while you cook the pasta (or longer if possible).

Cook the pasta according to the instructions on the package. Drain well and immediately stir in the fresh tomato sauce. Serve at once with the grated cheese.

Pasta is the archetypal fast food. This one is fast and fresh, with the ricotta melting into the hot pasta and coating it like a creamy sauce. The pine nuts give it crunch, while the herbs lend a fresh, scented flavour. If you don't have all the herbs listed here, use just rocket/arugula plus one other – the parsley or basil suggested, or perhaps snipped chives.

PASTA WITH MELTED RICOTTA
and herby parmesan sauce

350 g/12 oz. dried penne or other pasta

6 tablespoons/⅓ cup extra virgin olive oil

100 g/4 oz. (about 1 cup) pine nuts

125 g/4 oz. rocket/arugula, thinly sliced

2 tablespoons chopped fresh parsley

2 tablespoons chopped fresh basil

250 g/8 oz. fresh ricotta cheese, about 1 cup, mashed

50 g/4 oz. (about 1¼ cups) freshly grated Parmesan cheese

cracked black pepper

serves 4

Cook the pasta according to the instructions on the package.

Meanwhile, heat the olive oil in a frying pan/skillet, add the pine nuts and fry gently until golden. Set aside.

Drain the cooked pasta, reserving 4 tablespoons/¼ cup of the cooking liquid and return both to the pan. Add the pine nuts and their olive oil, the herbs, ricotta, half the Parmesan and plenty of cracked black pepper. Stir until evenly coated.

Serve in warmed bowls, with the remaining cheese sprinkled over.

SHRIMP FRIED RICE

2 tablespoons peanut or sunflower oil

2 garlic cloves, chopped

3 cm/1 inch fresh ginger, peeled and grated

1 fresh red chilli/chile, seeded and chopped

350 g/12 oz. small uncooked prawns/shrimp, peeled and deveined

250 g/10 oz. (about 2 cups) frozen peas, thawed

6 spring onions/scallions, trimmed and sliced

4 tablespoons/¼ cup Asian dried shrimp*

2 eggs, lightly beaten

800 g/5 cups cooked jasmine rice (from 350 g/1¾ cups uncooked rice)

3 tablespoons light soy sauce

freshly squeezed juice of ½ lemon

2 tablespoons chopped fresh coriander/cilantro

serves 4

Heat the oil in a wok and swirl to coat. Add the garlic, ginger and chilli/chile and stir-fry for 30 seconds. Add the prawns/shrimp, peas, spring onions/scallions and dried shrimp* and stir-fry for 2 minutes until the prawns/shrimp turn pink.

Using a spatula, push the mixture to one side, add the eggs and scramble until set. Then add the rice and stir over a high heat for 2 minutes until heated through.

Stir in the soy sauce, lemon juice and coriander/cilantro and serve.

*Note Asian dried shrimp are available in packages in Chinese markets. They keep very well in an airtight container if you don't use all of them.

COCONUT + LIME LEAF RICE

350 g/2 cups jasmine rice

350 ml/1½ cups coconut milk

12 lime leaves, bruised, or grated zest of 2 unwaxed limes

1 stalk of lemongrass, bruised

1 teaspoon sea salt

serves 6

Put the rice in a sieve/strainer and wash under cold running water until the water runs clear. Drain and shake well.

Put the rice, coconut milk, lime leaves, lemongrass and salt, and 350 ml/1½ cups water in a heavy saucepan. Bring to the boil, cover with a tight-fitting lid and simmer very gently for 20 minutes.

Remove the pan from the heat but leave undisturbed for a further 10 minutes. Fluff up with a fork and serve.

Adding a nip of vodka right at the end adds a delightful flavour to this risotto.
Although this recipe takes slightly longer than most in the book, it is simple to
make and always a terrific success with guests.

FENNEL + LEMON RISOTTO

a small pinch of saffron threads

1.25 kg/5 cups hot Vegetable Stock
(page 143)

1 large fennel bulb

125 g/1¼ sticks unsalted butter

1 onion, chopped

2 garlic cloves

juice and grated zest of 1 unwaxed
lemon

300 g/1½ cups risotto rice, such as
arborio

100 ml/½ cup vodka

50 g/¼ cup freshly grated Parmesan
cheese

sea salt and freshly ground black
pepper

serves 4

Soak the saffron in the hot stock until required. Finely chop the
fennel and the fronds.

Melt half the butter in a frying pan/skillet, add the onion, chopped
fennel, garlic and lemon zest, and fry gently for 10 minutes until
softened. Add the rice and stir for 30 seconds until the grains
are glossy.

Meanwhile, heat the saffron stock to a gentle simmer. Add a
ladle of the stock to the rice and cook, stirring until absorbed.
Continue adding the stock a little at a time, stirring and cook for
about 20 minutes until the liquid is absorbed and the rice is al
dente (just done).

Remove the pan from the heat, stir in remaining butter, lemon
juice, vodka, Parmesan, reserved fennel fronds, salt and pepper,
cover, leave for 5 minutes, then serve.

PIZZA
+ BREAD

By their very nature, pastry, pizza and bread doughs take time, but I did want to have some in the book. I love making them and there are many delicious breads that are relatively fast.

Making dough for pizzas is deceptive – although you should allow time for the dough to rise, the actual preparation and cooking time is short. I often make up a batch of dough, then go out to do the rest of the shopping. You can even leave it in a coolish place for the day, then punch it down just before baking. I have included three different pizza recipes and, if time is limited, you can use a package pizza dough mix or a frozen pizza base as an alternative.

The two bread recipes use dough that doesn't need to rise, drastically reducing the preparation time. The soda bread is a timeless classic, great served with soup and is also delicious toasted. The cornbread is spiked with chilli/chile and coriander/cilantro. It is wonderfully savoury, can be eaten warm and is also great toasted.

If you are really short of time you can cheat a little here and use a 500-g/16-oz. pack of frozen dough, cut in half – for two people you will need a whole package. Follow the instructions on the pack but let the dough rise for 15 minutes after you've rolled it out.

MOZZARELLA PIZZA
with garlic and rosemary

250 g/1⅔ cups plain/all-purpose flour, plus extra for dusting

1 teaspoon active dry yeast (½ a package)

1 teaspoon sea salt

1 tablespoon extra virgin olive oil, plus extra to serve

125–150 g/½–⅔ cup very warm water

TOPPING
250 g/8 oz. fresh mozzarella cheese, chopped

2 garlic cloves, sliced

2 sprigs of rosemary

sea salt and freshly ground black pepper

a pizza stone or baking sheet

serves 2–4

To make the dough, sift the flour into the bowl of a food mixer fitted with a dough hook attachment or a food processor fitted with a plastic blade. Add the yeast and salt, then work in the oil and water to form a soft dough.

Remove from the bowl and transfer to a floured work surface. Roll into a ball and put in an oiled bowl. Cover with clingfilm/plastic wrap and let rise for about 45 minutes or until doubled in size.

Preheat the oven to its highest setting, about 240°C (475°F) Gas 9 and put a pizza stone or baking sheet on the top shelf to heat.

Divide the risen dough in half and transfer one half to a well-floured surface. Roll it out to 30 cm/12 inches diameter. Take the hot stone or baking sheet from the oven and carefully put the pizza base on top. Spread with half the mozzarella, garlic and rosemary leaves, then season with salt and pepper and sprinkle with a little extra oil. Bake in the preheated oven for 10–12 minutes until bubbling and lightly golden. Repeat with the second pizza.

It is best to eat the pizzas as soon as they come out of the oven, so I recommend sharing each one as they are cooked.

If you are making fresh pizza bases, I recommend that you cook the pizzas one at a time and eat them as soon as they are ready (unless you have two ovens). Use the regular rather than convection setting on your oven to make sure that you have a good, crisp base on the pizza.

TOMATO PIZZA
with capers and anchovies

1 recipe Pizza Dough (page 107), 2 packs pizza base mix (200 g/ 6½ oz. each), or 1 pack frozen pizza dough (500 g/16 oz.), halved

plain/all-purpose flour, for dusting

2 large ripe tomatoes, chopped

2 tablespoons capers, rinsed and drained

12 anchovy fillets in oil, drained and chopped

250 g/8 oz. fresh mozzarella cheese, chopped

a few basil leaves

sea salt and freshly ground black pepper

a pizza stone or baking sheet

serves 2

If using pizza base mix, prepare the dough according to the directions on the package. Put the dough in a bowl and let rise until doubled in size.

Preheat the oven to its highest setting, about 240°C (475°F) Gas 9, and put a pizza stone or baking sheet on the top shelf to heat.

Divide the risen dough in half and transfer one half to a well-floured surface. Roll it out to 30 cm/12 inches diameter. Take the hot stone or baking sheet from the oven and carefully put the pizza base on top. Add half the tomatoes, capers, anchovies, mozzarella and a few basil leaves. Bake in the preheated oven for 10–12 minutes until bubbling and golden. Serve at once, then repeat to make a second pizza.

Not a pizza, not a tart, but halfway between the two and totally delicious. Usually, a pizza is cooked on a preheated pizza stone so that the base will be crisp. You can use a preheated baking sheet to achieve a good result.

MUSHROOM MASCARPONE PIZZA

1 recipe Pizza Dough (page 107), 2 packs pizza base mix (200 g/ 6½ oz. each), or 1 pack frozen pizza dough (500 g/16 oz.), halved

6 tablespoons extra virgin olive oil

2 garlic cloves, sliced

1 tablespoon chopped fresh thyme

500 g/1 lb. small open/cremini mushrooms, sliced

plain/all-purpose flour, for dusting

200 g/8 oz. mascarpone cheese

25 g/⅓ cup (about 1 oz.) freshly grated Parmesan cheese

sea salt and freshly ground black pepper

a pizza stone or baking sheet

serves 2–4

If using pizza base mix, prepare the dough according to the directions on the package. Transfer the dough to a bowl and let rise until doubled in size.

Preheat the oven to its highest setting, about 240°C (475°F) Gas 9, and put a pizza stone or baking sheet on the top shelf to heat.

Heat the oil in a frying pan/skillet and fry the garlic and thyme for 1 minute. Add the mushrooms and fry for a further 4–5 minutes until they are brown but haven't started to release their juices. Season with salt and pepper.

Divide the risen dough in half and transfer one half to a well-floured surface. Roll it out to 30 cm/12 inches diameter. Take the hot pizza stone or baking sheet from the oven and carefully put the pizza base on top. Spoon half the mushrooms on top and dot with half the mascarpone.

Sprinkle with half the Parmesan and bake in the preheated oven for 10–12 minutes until bubbling and golden. Serve at once and then repeat to make a second pizza.

The classic Irish soda bread is made with bicarbonate of/baking soda as the raising agent rather than yeast. This means the dough can be baked immediately, rather than having to let it rise as with a yeasted dough. Quick and easy to make.

SODA BREAD

400 g/2⅔ cups wholemeal/whole wheat flour, plus extra for dusting and sprinkling
1 teaspoon bicarbonate of/baking soda
1 teaspoon sea salt
1 teaspoon sugar
300 ml/1¼ cups buttermilk

a baking sheet, oiled
makes 1 small loaf

Put the flour, bicarbonate of/baking soda, salt, and sugar in a bowl and mix well. Make a well in the center, add the buttermilk, and gradually work it into the flour to make a soft dough.

Knead on a lightly floured surface for 5 minutes and then shape into a flattened round loaf. Transfer to an oiled baking sheet and, using a sharp knife, cut a cross in the top of the dough. Sprinkle with a little extra flour.

Bake in a preheated oven 230°C (450°F) Gas 8 for 15 minutes, then reduce the heat to 200°C (400°F) Gas 6 and bake for a further 30 minutes until risen and the loaf sounds hollow when tapped underneath.

Transfer to a wire rack and let cool completely.

I like to cook this cornbread in a deep loaf pan so later it can be sliced and toasted more easily. However, if you are short of time, pour the mixture into a greased baking pan lined on the bottom with baking parchment and cook for 20–25 minutes.

CHILLI/CHILE CORNBREAD

75 g/½ cup plain/all-purpose flour

1 tablespoon baking powder

200 g/1⅓ cups medium cornmeal or polenta

1 teaspoon sea salt

3 eggs, beaten

300 ml/1¼ cups buttermilk

4 tablespoons/¼ cup extra virgin olive oil

200 g/8 oz. (about 1 cup) canned corn kernels, drained

1–2 fresh red chillies/chiles, seeded and chopped

2 tablespoons chopped fresh coriander/cilantro

a deep loaf pan, 1 kg/2 lb., greased and bottom lined with parchment paper

serves 8–12

Sift the flour and baking powder into a bowl and stir in the cornmeal and salt.

Mix the eggs, buttermilk and oil in a second bowl then, using a wooden spoon, stir into the dry ingredients to make a smooth batter. Stir in the corn, chilli/chile, and coriander/cilantro and pour into the prepared loaf pan.

Bake in a preheated oven at 200°C (400°F) Gas 6 for 40 minutes. Let cool in the pan for 5 minutes, then remove from the pan and let cool on a wire rack.

DESSERTS + DRINKS

As a child I remember every main meal ended with a dessert, but today this seems to be something most of us reserve for a dinner party or at best the weekends. Time and health issues may be the reason for this, but not all sweet things have to be rich and heavy, and some don't take long to prepare. Good-quality fresh fruit needs little to adorn it – just pick flavours that work well together and combine them simply.

If your sweet tooth is utterly incorrigible, you will probably decide that chocolate is worth whatever time it takes, so I have included some drinks and desserts for you. Other 'proper desserts' take a little more time, but are worth every second, I'm sure you'll agree.

This book wouldn't be complete without a section on drinks and, although many drinks are already quick and simple to prepare (only a few seconds to open that chilled bottle of wine), I'm always on the lookout for new combinations – James Bondi is one of my favourites, now that I live in Sydney.

Strawberries and black pepper are surprisingly good partners. The orange flower water adds a lovely perfumed quality to the strawberries, but can be omitted.

STRAWBERRIES
with black pepper

500 g/1 lb. strawberries

1 tablespoon orange flower water
  (optional)

1 tablespoon caster/granulated sugar

2 teaspoons cracked black pepper

serves 4

Hull the strawberries and cut in half. Sprinkle with the orange flower water, if using, and with the sugar, and black pepper. Chill for 15 minutes and serve.

Note Strawberries should be washed and dried before hulling, not after, otherwise they fill up with water.

Rose water, like orange flower water, is sold in the baking section of supermarkets, in drugstores and in ethnic food stores specializing in Middle Eastern or Indian products.

RHUBARB COMPOTE
with yogurt

500 g/1 lb. rhubarb, trimmed

50 g/¼ cup sugar, or to taste

125 g/½ cup plain yogurt

1 tablespoon honey

½ tablespoon rose water

serves 4

Cut the rhubarb into 5 cm/2-inch slices and put in a saucepan. Add the sugar and 4 tablespoons/¼ cup water. Bring to the boil, cover and simmer gently for 15 minutes until the rhubarb has softened. Taste and stir in extra sugar if necessary. Transfer to a dish and let cool.

Put the yogurt, honey and rose water in a bowl, mix well then serve with the rhubarb.

Vanilla sugar is easy to make – just put a couple vanilla pods/beans
in a bottle of sugar and leave them there, topping up with fresh sugar
as necessary. You can use the beans for cooking, pat dry with paper
towels, then return to the sugar. If you don't have vanilla sugar, use
regular sugar and a drop of vanilla extract.

ROASTED PEACHES

4 large ripe peaches

2 tablespoons honey

150 g/8 oz. (about 1 cup) mascarpone
cheese

3 tablespoons vanilla sugar

1 tablespoon freshly squeezed lemon
juice

serves 4

Cut the peaches in half, remove the stones, and arrange the fruit
cut side up in a roasting pan. Pour over the honey and roast in a
preheated oven at 200°C (400°F) Gas 6 for about 20 minutes until
softened and lightly golden.

Mix the mascarpone with the vanilla sugar and lemon juice and
spoon onto the hot peaches. Serve at once.

Melon and ginger is a classic combination of flavours, and this simple
version is perfect for a warm summer's day. You can use any type of melon,
but my favourite is cantaloupe.

MELON WITH GINGER SYRUP

75 g/⅓ cup caster/granulated sugar

3 cm/1 inch fresh ginger, peeled and
finely chopped

freshly squeezed juice of ½ large
lemon

1 large ripe melon

serves 4 – 6

Put the sugar and 150 ml/⅔ cup water in a small saucepan and
heat gently to dissolve the sugar. Bring to the boil, add the ginger
and lemon juice and simmer gently for 3 minutes. Remove from
the heat and let cool.

Cut the melon into wedges, scoop out the seeds and serve
sprinkled with ginger syrup.

Fruit fritters are delicious and very simple to make. I serve them with cinnamon ice cream, available in some supermarkets and specialist food stores. Cinnamon and banana make an excellent flavour combination, but choose your own favourite flavour.

BANANA FRITTERS
with cinnamon ice cream

2 large bananas
cinnamon ice cream, to serve
ginger batter
40 g/⅓ cup plain/all-purpose flour
a pinch of sea salt
1 egg, separated
75 ml/⅓ cup ginger beer or sparkling water
1 tablespoon peanut or sunflower oil, plus extra for deep-frying

serves 4

Peel the bananas, cut into 4 chunks, then cut the chunks in half lengthways.

To make the batter, sift the flour and salt in a bowl, beat in the egg yolk, ginger beer or sparkling water and oil to form a smooth batter. Beat the egg white in a separate bowl until soft peaks form, then fold into the batter.

Heat 5 cm/2 inches of the oil in deep saucepan until it reaches 180°C (350°F) Gas 4 or until a cube of bread turns golden brown in 30 seconds.

Dip the banana chunks into the batter and deep-fry in batches of 3–4 for about 1 minute until the batter is crisp and golden. Drain on paper towels and keep the fritters warm in a moderate oven while you cook the remainder. Serve with a scoop of cinnamon ice cream.

...ead and butter pudding was one of my childhood favourites, and I couldn't have been happier than when it enjoyed a revival a few of years ago. Below is my version of this wonderful retro recipe, and if you make them in individual dishes, they will cook in under 20 minutes.

BREAD + BUTTER PUDDINGS

300 ml/1¼ cups milk

300 ml/1¼ cups double/heavy cream

½ teaspoon vanilla extract

4 tablespoons/¼ cup sugar

3 eggs

6 thick slices of brioche bread or hot cross buns, halved

50 g/2 oz. (about ⅓ cup) sultanas/ golden raisins

1 whole nutmeg

6 ramekins, 200 ml/1 cup each, well buttered

serves 6

Put the milk, cream, vanilla and 3 tablespoons of the sugar in a saucepan and heat until the sugar dissolves.

Put the eggs in a bowl, beat well, stir in 2–3 tablespoons of the hot milk mixture to warm the eggs, then stir in the remainder of the hot milk.

Lightly toast the slices of brioche and cut into quarters. Divide between the 6 prepared ramekins and sprinkle with the sultanas/ golden raisins.

Pour in the custard, grate a little nutmeg over the top, then sprinkle with the remaining tablespoon of sugar. Bake in a preheated oven at 180°C (350°F) Gas 4 for 18–20 minutes until firm.

Remove from the oven, let cool a little then serve warm.

Even if you never make desserts at any other time, you probably do when you have people to dinner. Perfect for a dinner party, these little plum fudge desserts can be prepared well ahead of time, then cooked just before serving.

PLUM FUDGE DESSERTS

50 g/4 tablespoons unsalted butter

50 g/4–5 tablespoons honey

2 tablespoons double/heavy cream

2 tablespoons brown sugar

1 teaspoon ground mixed/apple pie spice or a pinch of cinnamon plus a little freshly grated nutmeg

75 g/1½ cups fresh white bread crumbs

2 ripe plums, halved, stoned and thinly sliced

sour cream or crème fraîche, to serve

4 ramekins, 150 ml/⅔ cup each

serves 4

Put the butter, honey and cream in a saucepan and heat until melted. Put the sugar, spice and bread crumbs in a bowl and stir well.

Divide half the buttery fudge mixture between the ramekins and top with a layer of plum slices and half the bread crumb mix. Add the remaining plums and bread crumbs, then spoon over the remaining sauce.

Set on a baking sheet and bake in a preheated oven at 200°C (400°F) Gas 6 for 20 minutes. Remove from the oven and let cool for 5 minutes, then carefully unmould the desserts and serve with a spoonful of sour cream or crème fraîche.

...ate and rosemary may sound an unusual combination, but in fact the ...s go very well together. Remove the mousses from the refrigerator about 1 hour before serving so that they can return to room temperature.

CHOCOLATE + ROSEMARY POTS

300 ml/1¼ cups single/light cream

2 sprigs of rosemary, bruised, plus 6 extra, to serve (optional)

200 g/8 oz. dark/bittersweet chocolate, chopped

2 egg yolks

2 tablespoons unsalted butter

6 espresso cups or small ramekins

serves 6

Put the cream and rosemary sprigs in a saucepan and heat slowly just to boiling point. Remove from the heat and leave to infuse for 20 minutes.

Strain into a clean pan, add the chocolate and heat very gently until the chocolate melts – don't let the mixture boil. Remove from the heat, let cool slightly, then stir in the egg yolks one at a time. Finally add the butter, stirring until melted.

Pour the mixture into the espresso cups and let cool. Chill for 2 hours. Spear each chocolate pot with a rosemary sprig, if using, just before serving.

Brownies are everyone's favourite chocolate indulgence. They're not complicated to make, and the better the chocolate, the better they will be. The most important rule is to aim for the right texture – just set on top, but wonderfully gooey and melting on the inside. Most people can't resist eating them the minute they come out of the oven – plain or with a cup of coffee. But if you can wait, try them as a quick dessert, served with cream or ice cream.

CHOCOLATE + CINNAMON BROWNIES

75 g/½ cup (about 3 oz.) blanched hazelnuts,

275 g/10 oz. bittersweet chocolate (at least 70% cocoa solids)

225 g/2¼ sticks unsalted butter

3 eggs

225 g/1 cup plus 2 tablespoons caster/granulated sugar

75 g/½ cup self-raising/rising flour

2 teaspoons ground cinnamon

100 g/3 oz. white chocolate chips

a baking pan, 18 x 28 cm/9 x 13 inches, greased and bottom lined with parchment paper

serves 8–12

Put the hazelnuts in a dry frying pan/skillet and toast over medium heat until aromatic. Do not let burn. Let cool, then chop coarsely.

Put the chocolate and butter in a heatproof bowl set over a saucepan of simmering water and melt gently. Put the eggs and sugar in a bowl and beat until pale. Stir in the melted chocolate, flour, cinnamon, white chocolate chips and chopped hazelnuts.

Spoon into the prepared pan and bake in a preheated oven at 190°C (375°F) Gas 5 for 30–35 minutes until the top sets but the mixture still feels soft underneath.

Remove from the oven and let cool in the pan. Cut into squares to serve.

These pastry puffs filled with chocolate remind me of the delicious French pastry, pain au chocolat. Making them with frozen puff pastry dough is even faster than a trip to the pâtisserie. If you prefer, you can use plain dark chocolate instead of the white.

SPICED WHITE CHOCOLATE PUFFS

2 sheets ready-rolled puff pastry dough, thawed if frozen

plain/all-purpose flour, for dusting

175 g/8 oz. white chocolate, cut into 24 squares

1 teaspoon ground mixed/apple pie spice or a pinch of cinnamon plus a little freshly grated nutmeg

1 egg yolk

2 tablespoons milk

unsweetened cocoa powder, to serve

a baking sheet, greased

makes 8

Put the puff pastry dough on a floured work surface and cut each sheet into 4 pieces, 10 cm/4 inches square.

Put 3 pieces of chocolate onto each square, then add a light dusting of mixed/apple pie spice (I use a small tea strainer). Dampen the edges with a little water, then fold them over diagonally to form a triangle. Press the edges together to seal, then, using the blade of a sharp knife, gently tap the sealed edges several times (this will help the pastry rise).

Transfer the triangles to the baking sheet. Put the egg yolk and milk in a small bowl, beat well, then brush over the dough. Bake in a preheated oven at 220°C (425°F) Gas 7 for 10–15 minutes until risen and golden.

Remove from the oven, let cool for 5 minutes, lightly dust with cocoa powder and serve.

The perfect nightcap, sleepytime chocolate with a hint of romantic after-dinner mints – just the thing to send you off into a peaceful sleep, or warm you up on a chilly winter's afternoon.

MINTED HOT CHOCOLATE

600 ml/2¾ cups milk

4 sprigs of fresh mint, bruised lightly to extract flavour

50 g/2 oz. bittersweet chocolate, chopped

sugar, to taste (optional)

serves 2

Put the milk and mint sprigs in a saucepan and heat very gently until boiling. Boil for 1 minute, then remove from the heat. Discard the mint.

Divide the chocolate between 2 mugs. Stir in the milk and continue to stir until melted. Serve the sugar separately, if using.

Kids will love this shake, particularly with a spoonful of extra ice cream. I've made it optional, but of course it can't possibly be!

CHOCOLATE + BANANA CINNAMON SHAKE

2 bananas

4 scoops chocolate ice cream, plus extra to serve (optional)

300 ml/1¼ cups milk

1 teaspoon ground cinnamon

serves 4

Peel and chop the bananas. Put the ice cream, bananas, milk and cinnamon in a blender and purée until smooth. Pour into tall glasses and serve with an extra scoop of chocolate ice cream, if using.

Tisane is the French word for an infusion of herbs, flowers or other aromatics.
I think it's a beautiful word for this deliciously spicy drink, which I've chilled
down to make a great contrast between hot and cold.

CHILLED LEMONGRASS TISANE

1–2 fresh red chillies/chiles, seeded
  and sliced
2–4 stalks of lemongrass, outer leaves
  discarded, inner section finely sliced
5 cm/2 inches fresh ginger, peeled
  and sliced
50 g/¼ cup caster/granulated sugar
freshly squeezed juice of 2 lemons
mint leaves and ice cubes, to serve

serves 4

Put the chilli/chile in a heatproof bowl with the lemongrass, ginger
and sugar, then add 1 litre/1 quart boiling water and the lemon
juice and stir to dissolve the sugar. Set aside to infuse until it
reaches room temperature.

Strain the cooled liquid and chill for at least 30 minutes, then serve
in tall glasses with mint leaves and ice cubes.

My juicer has a citrus attachment as well as a juicer, so this drink couldn't be
simpler. If you don't have the citrus press, just peel the oranges and put them
through the regular juicer (don't forget to remove all the bitter white pith).

ORANGE AND APPLE REFRESHER

2 large oranges, peeled
2 Granny Smith apples
3 cm/1 inch fresh ginger, peeled
ice cubes, to serve

a juicing machine
serves 2

Push the oranges, apples and ginger through the juicer. Half-fill 2
tall glasses with ice cubes, pour the juice over the top and serve.

This is a variation on the classic champagne cocktail I found at a funky Sydney bar, beside the famous beach that inspired the pun.

JAMES BONDI

6 brown sugar lumps
60 ml/¼ cup vodka
a dash of Angostura bitters
1 bottle chilled champagne

serves 6

Put the sugar lumps in 6 champagne flutes, add the vodka and stir with a spoon until the sugar completely dissolves (crush it slightly if necessary).

Add a dash of bitters to each one, top up with champagne and serve.

Campari and grapefruit juice are a marriage made in heaven, lovely with or without sugar.

CAMPARI GRAPEFRUIT SLUSH

600 ml/2¾ cups ice cubes
100 ml/¼ cup Campari
200 ml/¾ cup ruby grapefruit juice
sugar, to taste

serves 4

Put the ice cubes in a blender and grind until crushed. Add the Campari and grapefruit juice and blend until slushy. Add sugar to taste. Serve in chilled glasses with short cocktail straws.

A white wine variation of the more classic Spanish aperitif, cool and delightful on a hot summer's day.

PEACH SANGRIA

1 bottle chilled dry white wine
4 tablespoons/¼ cup peach liqueur
4 large ripe peaches, sliced
1 orange, sliced
1 unwaxed lemon, sliced
ice cubes
chilled lemonade

serves 6

Pour the wine in a large jug/pitcher, then add the peach liqueur, sliced peaches, orange and lemon. Add ice cubes and stir well. When ready to serve, half-fill tall glasses with ice cubes, wine and fruit, then top up with the lemonade.

THE BASICS:
Flavoured oils, butters and dressings

OILS

Herbs, spices and aromatics can all be added to oils to enhance the flavour and provide another valuable staple for the storecupboard. They should be infused in the oil for about 7 days for the best results. Heating the oil and flavourings over a gentle heat speeds up the process as well as killing off any harmful bacteria. It is always best to strain the oil after the flavours have developed, then store in a cool place.

Another method of flavouring oil is to purée the herb and oil, then strain off the residue. This gives a vibrant green oil with a lovely flavour. As well as recipes for Fragrant Garlic Oil (page 21), Basil Oil (page 26), here are:

Thyme Oil

6 sprigs of fresh thyme
600 ml/2¾ cups extra virgin olive oil

makes 600 ml/2¾ cups

Lightly crush the thyme sprigs with a rolling pin to help release the aromas and put in a screw-top bottle. Add the oil and leave to infuse for at least 7 days. Strain into a clean bottle and use as required.

Chilli/Chili Oil

300 ml/1¼ cups extra virgin olive oil
4 dried red chillies/chilies, coarsely chopped

makes 300 ml/1¼ cups

Put the oil and chillies/chilies in a screw-top bottle and leave to infuse for 2 days before using.

BUTTERS

Flavouring butter with spices and herbs is great fun as well as cost effective – just think of the amount of herbs you throw away when you have chopped up a few too many. There are so many different combinations of flavours you can use. Try Horseradish and Chive (page 80), or one of the following:

Mustard and Tarragon Butter

2 tablespoons chopped fresh tarragon leaves
1 tablespoon whole grain mustard
125 g/1¼ sticks unsalted butter, softened

makes 125 g/4 oz.

Beat the tarragon and mustard into the butter. Roll into a small log, wrap in clingfilm/plastic wrap and freeze until required.

Coriander/cilantro, Lime and Pepper Butter

2 tablespoons chopped fresh coriander/cilantro
125 g/1¼ sticks unsalted butter, softened
grated zest and juice of 1 unwaxed lime
½ teaspoon cracked black pepper

makes 125 g/4 oz.

Finely chop the coriander/cilantro, then beat into the butter with the remaining ingredients. Roll, wrap and freeze, as above.

Mint and Cumin Butter

Although this is a great partner for lamb chops, I also like it tossed with cooked baby new potatoes and left for a few minutes to infuse.

½ tablespoon cumin seeds

2 tablespoons chopped fresh mint

125 g/1¼ sticks unsalted butter, softened

makes 125 g/4 oz.

Toast the cumin seeds in a dry frying pan/skillet for about 3 minutes until they start to 'pop' and release their aromas. Cool, then crush using a pestle and mortar.

Finely chop the mint leaves and beat into the butter with the cumin seeds. Roll, wrap and freeze, as above.

DRESSINGS

I always like to keep a jar of homemade dressing in the refrigerator so that making a salad for lunch takes just a few minutes. If the dressing includes herbs, it is best made just before you use it – or make up the dressing, but leave the herbs until the last minute. You'll find other dressing recipes throughout the book – Lemon and Coriander/Cilantro (page 55), Black Bean (page 31), and others – but here are some of my favourites:

Classic French Dressing

150 ml/⅔ cup extra virgin olive oil

2 tablespoons white wine vinegar

2 teaspoons Dijon mustard

½ teaspoon sugar

sea salt and freshly ground black pepper

makes 175 ml/¾ cup

Put all the ingredients into screw-top bottle and shake vigorously until amalgamated. Store in the refrigerator and shake again before using.

Salmoriglio

This Italian dressing is served with grilled/broiled fish or chicken – I love it with red mullet or bream. Look out for the sweet Italian-style lemons now more widely available.

200 ml/¾ cup extra virgin olive oil

freshly squeezed juice of 1 large lemon

2 tablespoons chopped fresh parsley

2 garlic cloves, crushed

a pinch of dried oregano

sea salt and freshly ground black pepper

makes 225 ml/1 cup

Put all the ingredients into a screw-top bottle and shake well. Serve the same day.

Reduced Balsamic Vinegar

Reducing a cheap balsamic vinegar produces a sauce almost as good as an aged balsamic, which would cost a great deal more. It may seem like a terrible waste simply to boil away the vinegar but the resulting thick glaze can be used sparingly and will provide a delicious finish to many dishes.

300 ml/1¼ cups balsamic vinegar

makes 100 ml/½ cup

Put the vinegar in a small saucepan and boil gently until it is reduced by two-thirds and reaches the consistency of thick syrup. Let cool, then store in a clean bottle.

SAUCES AND STOCKS

SAUCES

Many useful sauces, such as Wasabi Mayonnaise (page 14) or Pistachio and Mint Pesto (page 50), appear in this book. Others include:

Mayonnaise

Some extra virgin olive oils can make this sauce slightly bitter, so I use a gentler oil such as French or Spanish. You can also use a mixture of extra virgin and pure olive oils.

2 egg yolks
2 teaspoons white wine vinegar or lemon juice
¼ teaspoon salt
2 teaspoons Dijon mustard
300 ml/1¼ cups extra virgin olive oil
freshly ground black pepper

makes about 300 ml/1¼ cups

Put the egg yolks, vinegar or lemon juice, salt and mustard in a food processor and blend briefly until frothy. With the blade running drizzle the oil in through the funnel until the sauce is thick and glossy. It may be necessary to thin the mayonnaise slightly by blending in 1–2 tablespoons boiling water. Season to taste. To store in the refrigerator for up to 5 days, cover the surface with clingfilm/plastic wrap.

Quick Tomato Sauce

A simple, quick, delicious sauce to be tossed through pasta, spread over a pizza base or used as the base for a chicken or bean stew.

800 g/2 cans chopped tomatoes (400 g/15 oz. each)
4 garlic cloves, crushed
4 tablespoons/¼ cup extra virgin olive oil
1 teaspoon caster/granulated sugar
1 teaspoon dried oregano
2 tablespoons chopped fresh basil
sea salt and freshly ground black pepper

serves 4–6

Put the tomatoes, garlic, oil, sugar, oregano, salt and pepper in a saucepan. Bring to the boil and simmer, covered, over gentle heat for 30 minutes until reduced and well flavoured. Stir in the basil, and salt and pepper to taste. Serve, or cool and refrigerate overnight.

Quick Romesco Sauce

The traditional method for this Catalan sauce includes a dried red pepper, rather than paprika.

50 g/2 oz. blanched almonds
3 garlic cloves, chopped
75 ml/⅓ cup extra virgin olive oil
2 ripe tomatoes, coarsely chopped
2 tablespoons red wine vinegar
2 teaspoons smoked paprika
1 teaspoon caster/granulated sugar
½–1 teaspoon chilli/chili powder
sea salt

makes 300 ml/1¼ cups

Put the almonds in a dry frying pan/skillet and fry over medium heat until browned. Cool, then transfer to a food processor, add the garlic and blend briefly until coarsely ground.

Add the remaining ingredients, purée until fairly smooth, then season to taste. Store in the refrigerator for up to 3 days.

Almond and Parsley Pesto

This variation of regular basil pesto can be tossed through pasta, served with chicken or even used as a dip for bread.

50 g/2 oz. (about ½ cup) blanched almonds
25 g/1 oz. (about ¼ cup) pine nuts
a large bunch of flat-leaf parsley
2 garlic cloves, chopped
175 ml/¾ cup extra virgin olive oil
2 tablespoons freshly grated Parmesan cheese
sea salt and freshly ground black pepper

makes about 300 ml/1¼ cups

Put the almonds in a dry frying pan/skillet and fry over medium heat until browned, transfer to a bowl. Repeat with the pine nuts and let cool.

Put the nuts in a food processor, add the parsley and garlic and blend briefly. Add the oil and purée until smooth and vibrantly green. Stir in the cheese and season to taste. Store in the refrigerator for up to 5 days.

Chicken Stock

1 kg/2 lb. chicken backs and wings
2 carrots, coarsely chopped
3 celery stalks, coarsely chopped
1 onion, chopped
1 leek, chopped
6 garlic cloves, chopped
2 tomatoes, coarsely chopped
2 fresh bay leaves
2 sprigs of fresh thyme
6 white peppercorns
1 teaspoon salt

makes about 1.5 litres/6 cups

Put all the ingredients in a saucepan and cover with about 2 litres/2 quarts water. Bring to the boil, skim off the foam and simmer gently, uncovered, for 1 hour.

Pour through a fine sieve/strainer and let cool completely. Refrigerate until required or freeze for up to 3 months.

Fish Stock

1 kg/2 lb. fish trimmings/frames
900 ml/4 cups dry white wine
2 carrots, coarsely chopped
2 celery stalks, coarsely chopped
1 onion, chopped
1 leek, sliced
1 garlic clove, chopped
2 fresh bay leaves
2 sprigs of parsley
6 white peppercorns
1 teaspoon salt

makes about 900 ml/4 cups

Wash the fish trimmings and put in a large saucepan with all the remaining ingredients.

Add 900 ml/4 cups water, bring to the boil, skim off the foam and simmer gently for 30 minutes.

Strain in a clean pan and simmer until the stock is reduced to about 4 cups. Let cool completely and refrigerate until required or freeze for up to 3 months.

STOCKS

Though recipes in this book are fast and fresh, I include recipes for three basic stocks – make them when you have time and freeze them for later. You can also buy fresh stocks, but if you use stock cubes, look for the organic type, which have better flavour.

Vegetable Stock

2 onions, chopped
2 potatoes, chopped
2 leeks, sliced
4 carrots, sliced
1 large celery stalk, sliced
4 tomatoes, chopped
150 g/6 oz. mushrooms, chopped
4 garlic cloves, chopped

50 g/¼ cup rice or green lentils
150 ml/⅔ cup dry white wine
4 sprigs of parsley
2 sprigs of thyme
2 teaspoons sea salt
1 teaspoon black pepper

makes about 1.5 litres/6 cups

Put all the ingredients in a saucepan and add 1.75 litres/ 7 cups water. Bring to the boil, cover, and simmer for 1 hour.

Pour through a fine sieve/strainer and taste. Reduce the stock by simmering gently to enhance the flavour.

Refrigerate up to 3 days or freeze for up to 3 months.

INDEX

apples: orange & apple refresher 136
    pork steaks with apple & blackberry compote 87
asparagus grilled with goats' cheese & herb oil 43
avocado salsa 69

bananas: banana fritters with cinnamon ice cream 123
    chocolate & banana cinnamon shake 135
beans: lima beans with quick tomato sauce 32
    pan-fried chicken, creamy beans & leeks 72
    quick vegetarian mole 31
    white bean soup 32
beef: Japanese beef tataki 79
    pan-fried fillet steak with horseradish & chive butter 80
bread: chilli cornbread 115
    individual bread & butter puddings 124
    lamb in pitta bread 83
    soda bread 112
brownies, chocolate & cinnamon 131
butters, flavoured 140

cabbage, stir-fried sesame 25
Campari grapefruit slush 139
cheese 34
    cheese on toast 44
    figs with marinated feta 44
    homemade herb cheese 14
    mozzarella pizza with garlic & rosemary 107
    mushroom & mascarpone pizza 111
    pasta with melted ricotta 98
    roasted mascarpone peaches 120
    tomato pizza with capers & anchovies 108
    see also goats' cheese & chévre
chèvre, baked 43
chicken: chicken & garlic chive noodles 90
    chicken, lemon & yogurt skewers 17
    garlic-roasted birds 75
    jerk chicken wings with avocado salsa 69
    pan-fried chicken with creamy beans & leeks 72
    roast five-spice chicken with ginger bok choy 71
chillies/chiles: chilli cornbread 115
    chilli jam 10
    chilli oil 140
    pasta with chilli tuna tartare 94
    shrimp with chili oil 50
chocolate: chocolate & banana cinnamon shake 135
    chocolate & cinnamon brownies 131
    chocolate & rosemary pots 128
    minted hot chocolate 135
    quick vegetarian mole 31

spiced white chocolate puffs 132
clams, drunken 53
coconut & lime leaf rice 101
cornbread, chilli 115
couscous salad 21
curries: curried red lentils 28
    quick vegetable curry 25

drunken clams 53
duck with cinnamon-spiced plums 76

eggs, 34
    baked eggs with smoked salmon & chives 36
    frittata with fresh herbs & ricotta 40
    scrambled eggs with mushrooms 39

fennel: fennel, lemon & vodka risotto 102
    lobster & shaved fennel salad 54
figs with marinated feta 44
frittata with fresh herbs & ricotta 40
fritters, banana 123
fudge desserts, plum 127

garlic-roasted birds 75
goats' cheese: baked 43
    grilled asparagus with herb oil & 43
    warm soufflés 47
grapefruit slush, Campari,139

James Bondi 139
Japanese beef tataki 79
jerk chicken wings 69

lamb in pitta bread 83
lemon: lemon & coriander dressing 57
    salmoriglio 141
lemongrass tisane 136
lentils: curried red lentils 28
    spinach & lentil salad 84
lobster & shaved fennel salad 54

melon with ginger syrup 120
mole, quick vegetarian 31
monkfish, blackened 61
mozzarella pizza 107
mushrooms: mushroom & mascarpone pizza 111
    scrambled eggs with 39
mustard and tarragon butter 140
noodles: chicken & garlic chive noodles 90
    udon noodles with seven-spice salmon 93
oils, flavoured 140
olives: simple tomato & olive tart 26
orange & apple refresher 136

Prosciutto pork 84
parsley & almond pesto 142
pasta, 89–103
    with chilli tuna tartare 94
    with melted ricotta 98

with raw tomato sauce 97
pastries: spiced white chocolate puffs 132
pea & mint soup 22
pea sprout salad 14
peaches: peach sangria 139
    roasted mascarpone peaches 120
pistachio & mint pesto 50
pitta bread, lamb in 83
pizzas 104
    mozzarella with garlic & rosemary 107
    mushroom & mascarpone 111
    tomato with capers & anchovies 108
plums: duck with cinnamon-spiced plums 76
    plum fudge puddings 127
pork fillet 84
pork steaks with apple & blackberry compote 87
prawns/shrimp: shrimp with chilli oil 50
    shrimp fried rice 101
    Thai shrimp cakes 10

rhubarb compote with yogurt 119
rice: coconut & lime leaf rice 101
    fennel, lemon & vodka risotto 102
    shrimp fried rice 101
romesco sauce 142

salads: fragrant herb couscous 21
    lobster & shaved fennel 54
    pea sprout 14
    spinach & lentil 84
salmon: seared salmon with cucumber pickle 62
    udon noodles with seven-spice salmon 93
    baked eggs with chives & smoked 36
    smoked salmon bruschetta 13
salmoriglio 141
scallops with crushed potatoes 58
shrimp fried rice 101
soda bread 112
soufflés, warm goats' cheese 47
soups: pea & mint 22
    white bean with olive gremolata 32
spinach & lentil salad,84
squid with lemon & coriander dressing 57
strawberries with pepper 119
swordfish with new potatoes, beans & olives 65

tart, simple tomato & olive 26
Thai shrimp cakes 10
thyme oil 140
tofu stir-fried with chilli coconut sauce 22
tomatoes: lima beans with quick tomato sauce 32
    pasta with raw tomato sauce 97
    quick romesco sauce 142
    quick tomato sauce 142
    quick vegetarian mole 31
    simple tomato & olive tart 26
    tomato pizza with capers & anchovies 108

udon noodles with seven-spice salmon 93